MEALS FOR ME

MEALS FOR ME

ONE CORE
INGREDIENT

——

TWO DELICIOUS
MEALS

SAM STERN

Photography by Lisa Linder

QUADRILLE

Publishing Director: *Sarah Lavelle*
Creative Director: *Helen Lewis*
Senior Editor: *Céline Hughes*
Designer: *Gemma Hayden*
Photographer: *Lisa Linder*
Food Stylists: *Emily Jonzen and Aya Nishimura*
Prop Stylist: *Polly Webb-Wilson*
Production: *Emily Noto and Vincent Smith*

First published in 2015 by
Quadrille Publishing

Quadrille is an imprint of Hardie Grant
www.hardiegrant.com.au

Quadrille Publishing
Pentagon House
52–54 Southwark Street
London SE1 1UN
www.quadrille.co.uk

Text © 2015 Sam Stern
Photography © 2015 Lisa Linder
Design and layout © 2015 Quadrille
Publishing

Cataloguing in Publication Data: a catalogue record for
this book is available from the British Library.

ISBN: 978 184949 734 3

Printed in China

www.cooked.com

10 9 8 7 6 5 4 3 2 1

A note on the recipes:

Timings are guidelines for conventional ovens.
If you are using a convection (fan-assisted) oven,
set your oven temperature approximately 50 °F
[15 °C] lower. Use an oven thermometer to check
the temperature.

CONTENTS

6   INTRODUCTION

12   COOK CHICKEN

40   COOK DUCK

54   COOK BEEF

82   COOK PORK

106   COOK LAMB

128   COOK FISH

146   COOK VEGETABLES

172   SWEET TREATS

186   INDEX

192   ACKNOWLEDGMENTS

SENSATIONAL  SUPPERS

This book is about being creative in the kitchen, cooking what you love, and not having to please anyone else! Solo cooks should revel in having the kitchen exclusively to themselves; they shouldn't view it as a solitary experience but a real chance to have fun and experiment. In showing you how to cook for yourself, I hope to be able to inspire you to make the effort —and it's not even a big effort! It's exciting, and much more so than just chucking a couple of boring slices of bread in the toaster. With a bit of guidance, you'll soon get back into the joys of really good food.

The winning idea of this book is that you can make two different dishes from one core ingredient: by cooking the main recipe you are halfway to preparing another, which you can enjoy the next day and even take to work in a lunchbox. This not only saves you loads of time but it also makes financial sense. How often are you left with a lonely chicken breast in the package and no clue what to do with it the next day? You end up making the same thing again, right? But no one wants to eat the same thing over and over. I want to show you how to solve that problem, and turn it into something different and just as tasty to eat tomorrow.

Sometimes it's also much easier and more economical to buy a whole joint or bird and turn that value-for-money, grocery-store offer into a real bargain by creating four separate dishes that will last you over half the week—look for the Big Cook recipes. This is something I often do myself, and in this book, I'll show you how. There's no magic to it. You can fit it into any routine, whether that means picking bits up from the store on the way home from work, or booking in a big online delivery and using your refrigerator/freezer space.

In this book I'll share delicious recipes that are perfect for anyone dining alone, whether that means something quick and easy, or comforting and indulgent. There are some fantastic leftover options, too. Cooking for one shouldn't be apologetic—it's a celebration. For me, whether I've got a house full of people or I'm on my own for the night, I always like to make something delicious to eat. Cooking for yourself gives you more freedom. You are cook and critic. So with only yourself to please, and a stack of great recipes to choose from, you're bound to get rave reviews.

SAM

Kitchen
ESSENTIALS

Of course you can pick up groceries on your way home, or plan ahead at the weekend, but a well-stocked pantry (and freezer) makes life easy and means a delicious dinner is never too far away. These are my personal recommendations, but you can pick and choose your own favorites.

 ## HERBS & SPICES

Sea salt (recommend kosher)
Fine salt
Black pepper
Vanilla extract
Chinese five-spice
Ground cinnamon
Ground turmeric
Ground cumin
Garam masala
Curry powder
Ground coriander
Nutmeg: whole or ground
Mixed spice
Dried red pepper flakes
Chili powder
Cayenne pepper
Paprika: plain, smoked, sweet
Ground ginger
Dried herbs: oregano, mint, rosemary, thyme

 ## OILS

Olive (for cooking)
Extra virgin olive or canola (for salads)
Peanut (for stir-fries)
Sunflower (for frying/baking)

MUSTARDS

English
Dijon
Whole grain

VINEGARS

Chinese rice
Red and/or white
Cider
Balsamic

Capers
Olives
Chinese rice wine
Coconut milk
Mayonnaise
Tomato ketchup
Brown sauce
Worcestershire sauce
Thai fish sauce
Chili sauce
Hoisin sauce
Oyster sauce
Soy sauce: light and/or dark
Rose harissa paste
Curry paste (I use Patak's)
Red currant jelly
Light corn syrup
Honey
Maple syrup
Garbanzo beans (chickpeas)
Tomatoes: chopped in a can, pureed
Roasted red bell peppers in a jar
Broth
Couscous (I prefer whole wheat)
Cornmeal
Lentils
Dried pasta
Noodles
Flour
Baking powder
Baking soda
Oats

Beans

Baked
Haricot
Cannellini
Lima
Refried

SUGARS

Granulated
Superfine
Soft brown
Powdered

FOR YOUR FREEZER

Herbs
Chopped spinach
Peas
Berries
Bread: sliced, pita, wraps
Broth and wine frozen in ice-cube trays
Shrimp
Squid

Have FUN and EXPERIMENT

Handy tips
FOR BUYING AND STORING CORE INGREDIENTS

 ## CHICKEN

When buying a whole chicken, look for one that's fat, well-rounded, and neatly shaped. Its skin wants to be creamy and pretty uniformly smooth. Avoid anything with tears, marks, stubble, or marks from freezer burn. Check the packaging, too—it should be unscathed. Press before you buy: a properly stored bird should feel cold. Wrap it up in an extra bag when you take it home.

Store raw chicken in the refrigerator as soon as you get it home—as quickly as possible! Store it in the original packaging or, if opened, on a plate and loosely covered. Keep it away from other foods, especially cooked food. Fresh meat lasts up to 2 days. Top organic meat from the butcher can last 4 days. Follow sell-by dates.

 ## BEEF

When buying beef, check the color. You want a deep red with a network or marbling of creamy white fat throughout. It's an indicator of quality, a tender juiciness, and flavor to come. If it looks gray, slimy, or a uniform bright red color then avoid it. The fat should be creamy white.

Store raw beef in the refrigerator: take off any outer wrapping and store it on a plate, loosely covered, in the refrigerator away from cooked stuff. Meat lasts 3 to 5 days in the refrigerator. Cook ground beef within 24 hours.

 ## PORK

When buying pork, look for skin that's dry and smooth; meat that's pink and firm without a damp or oily sheen; fat that's white and thick; joints with a good layering of fat (it conducts heat to the skin which helps make great crackling). Avoid meat that looks slippery, and yellow fat.

Store raw pork in the refrigerator as soon as you get it home: keep it in its original plastic wrapped tray. If it's wrapped in butcher's paper, remove it to a plate and cover it with foil or wax paper. When a package of bacon has been opened, wrap it or store it in a container. Keep raw pork, bacon, and sausages away from cooked and fresh foods.

 # LAMB

When buying lamb, look for good marbling, a firm-textured meat with a pinkish hue, and firm white fat. Avoid it if the meat looks dark and wet, if there's too much fat, or if the fat is yellow and soft.

Store raw lamb in the refrigerator: keep it in its original sealed container. Transfer open or loosely wrapped lamb to a plate and cover loosely in foil or wax paper. Store away from cooked and raw foods. Refrigerate roasts, steaks, and chops for 3 to 5 days; diced meat for 2 days; ground lamb for 1 day.

 # FISH

When buying fillets of fresh white fish, the flesh should be white and translucent. Smoked fish should be glossy. Raw shrimp should be firm and glistening, with no black age spots. For mussels, try to get ones with cleaner, undamaged shells (not caked in mud or covered in barnacles).

Store fresh fish in the refrigerator as soon as you get it home—as quickly as possible! Make sure you store it at 32 to 41°F [0 to 5°C] and eat it within 24 hours of buying. Leave packaged fish in its container, and keep smoked fish well sealed so it doesn't flavor other foods. Let fish return to room temperature for 30 minutes before cooking.

 # RICE

Make sure leftover cooked rice cools rapidly (don't let it sit in a hot pan) and then refrigerate it immediately so it's safe to use. Don't leave it around at room temperature—the longer it stands like this, the more chance of food poisoning from bacteria formed on the cooked rice. Eat cooked rice within 24 hours.

EXTRA!

Cool hot food down before refrigerating it and make sure it is well wrapped.
Dishes such as curry, stews, and casseroles all benefit from chilling for a day or two.

COOK

CHICKEN

BEER AND ORANGE CHICKEN

First off: here's a simple, one-pot, Asian-style dish that I promise you will adore. A light beer works best to create a flavor-packed sauce that absorbs beautifully into the mushrooms and chicken. Second up we have a light summer salad. Bulk it up with leftovers, like Boston lettuce or radishes, tomatoes, etc.

Drizzle of peanut oil
4 chicken thighs, skin on and bone in
¾-in [2-cm] piece of ginger, peeled and cut into thin strips
7 Tbsp [100 ml] orange juice
⅝ cup [150 ml] beer (preferably a light lager)
1 Tbsp dark soy sauce
½ star anise
1 pack [8¾ oz/250 g] shiitake mushrooms
About 2¼ oz [60 g] egg noodles

2 FOR 1

BUY 4 CHICKEN THIGHS, COOK THEM IN THE FIRST RECIPE, AND USE THE LEFTOVERS IN THE NEXT RECIPE.

Put the peanut oil in a heavy-bottom saucepan or Dutch oven over medium heat. Add the chicken thighs and brown on both sides.

Pour the excess fat out of the pan, then add the ginger, and fry for 30 seconds. Add the orange juice, beer, soy sauce, and star anise and bring to a boil. Cover and simmer for 15 minutes.

Meanwhile, prepare the mushrooms by brushing them lightly with paper towel to remove any dirt and then slicing them into ⅜-in [1-cm] thick pieces. After the 15 minutes, add the mushrooms to the pan and cook for 5 minutes, covered but stirring occasionally. Prepare the egg noodles according to the package directions.

For crispy skin, pick the chicken thighs out of the pan and dry the skin with a paper towel. Place skin side down in a dry frying pan over medium heat, or pop under a hot broiler until the skin is crisp.

To serve, place your noodles in a bowl or plate, spoon on the mushrooms and cooking liquor, and add 2 of the chicken thighs. Let the remaining chicken thighs cool, then cover and refrigerate until ready to use in the next recipe.

ASIAN CHICKEN SALAD

2 leftover cooked chicken thighs from recipe above
4-in [10-cm] piece of cucumber
2 scallions
1 Tbsp dark soy sauce
1½ Tbsp sweet chili sauce
1 Tbsp rice wine vinegar
Splash of peanut oil
Fresh mint and cilantro, to serve

Remove the bone and any gristle from the cooked chicken thighs. Slice into ⅜-in [1-cm] thick pieces. Slice the cucumber into thin sticks. Chop the scallions into ¼-in [½-cm] chunks.

Mix together the soy sauce, chili sauce, vinegar, and peanut oil to form the dressing. Taste and adjust to your liking by adding more of anything. Plate up the cucumber, then the chicken and scallions, some mint and cilantro leaves, and finally drizzle on the dressing.

CHICKEN TERIYAKI

Chicken thighs are packed with such incredible flavor, and combined with dark, sweet Japanese teriyaki sauce, they are a real winner. The pickles are there to cut through the rich sweetness of the chicken. Surprisingly, this flavoring also works fantastically with nachos, which are perfect for pigging out on while watching TV. (Or you could make your colleagues jealous by including it in a lunchbox.)

4 chicken thighs, skin on (bone in
    or boneless—see method below)
About ⅓ cup [60 g] white or
    brown rice
Peanut or vegetable oil, for frying

Pickles
3 Tbsp rice vinegar
1 Tbsp water
5 tsp superfine sugar
Pinch of salt
1 carrot
2 pieces of Chinese leaf

Teriyaki marinade
2 Tbsp dark soy sauce
2 Tbsp mirin
1 Tbsp sake or rice wine
1 Tbsp honey

For the pickles, put the rice vinegar, water, sugar, and salt in a bowl. Stir well to dissolve the sugar and salt. Peel and slice the carrot into thin strips or semicircles about ⅛ in [¼ cm] thick. Slice the Chinese leaf to a similar thickness. Place both in the pickle bowl, give them a good mix, cover, and marinate for at least 30 minutes.

Now mix the teriyaki marinade ingredients in a bowl.

If your chicken thighs have their bones, remove the bone by cutting through the flesh along both sides of the bone with a sharp knife. Then slice underneath the bone and pull it out. Prick the thighs all over with the knife. Place in the marinade and leave for at least 20 minutes (the longer the better).

Preheat the oven to 400°F [200 °C].

Remove the marinated chicken from the bowl and dry the skin thoroughly with paper towels. Set aside the marinade.

Heat a dash of peanut or vegetable oil in an ovenproof frying pan over medium-low heat. Place the chicken in, skin side down, and cook until the skin crisps, taking care not to let it burn. Once crisp, transfer to the oven and cook for 15 minutes, or until cooked through. Meanwhile, prepare the rice according to the package directions.

Carefully remove the chicken pan from the oven and place it over very low heat on the stove. Tip in the marinade and cook for 30 seconds, or until it bubbles away.

Let the chicken rest for a few minutes, then slice up 2 of the thighs. Serve on top of the rice in a bowl and spoon over the teriyaki sauce. Add some pickles and get stuck in. Let the remaining chicken thighs cool, then cover and refrigerate until ready to use in the next recipe.

2 FOR 1

BUY 4 CHICKEN THIGHS, COOK THEM IN THE FIRST RECIPE, AND USE THE LEFTOVERS IN THE NEXT RECIPE.

CHICKEN AND CHEESE NACHOS

2 leftover cooked chicken thighs from recipe left
1½ oz [40 g] lightly salted nachos
Scant ¼ cup [25 g] grated cheddar cheese
2 tomatoes, diced
1 avocado, sliced
Small handful of fresh cilantro, torn
Dollop of sour cream (optional)

Preheat the oven to 400 °F [200 °C].

Slice the chicken into thin strips. Pile the nachos and chicken into an ovenproof dish and top with the grated cheddar. Bake in the preheated oven for 10 minutes. Pile into a bowl with the tomatoes, avocado, torn cilantro, and sour cream, if using. Get messy!

CHICKEN SAAG CURRY

This curry is a great takeout favorite, but even better for being homemade. Using frozen chopped spinach means that you'll only use what you actually need and the rest can go back in the freezer; this a great way of preventing waste. Be aware that the secret of succulent, tasty chicken is marinating—for at least 2 hours, or overnight. The recipe that follows is a healthy kabob—words that don't sit easily together, but it's true!

2 chicken breasts
Glug of peanut oil
1 medium red onion, thinly sliced
Pinch of salt
2 garlic cloves, crushed
1¼-in [3-cm] piece of ginger, peeled and grated
1 to 2 tsp tikka masala paste (I use Patak's)
14-oz [400-g] can chopped tomatoes
5 balls of frozen chopped spinach
About ⅓ cup [60 g] white rice
1 to 2 chapatis
Raita, to serve

Marinade
2 Tbsp tikka masala paste (I use Patak's)
3 garlic cloves, crushed
1¼-in [3-cm] piece of ginger, peeled and grated
Juice of ½ lemon
2 Tbsp plain yogurt

Chop the chicken into bite-size chunks. Mix together the marinade ingredients in a bowl and add the chicken. Cover and marinate in the refrigerator for between 2 and 24 hours. The longer you leave it, the better the flavor.

When the chicken has marinated, heat the peanut oil in a medium frying pan over low heat. Add the red onion and salt and slowly sweat until the onions start to turn golden brown. Add the garlic and ginger and cook for another 1 to 2 minutes, stirring as you go. Add the tikka masala paste and cook for another minute or so. Add the chopped tomatoes and cook gently for another 2 to 3 minutes.

Meanwhile, prepare the rice according to the package directions.

Put half the marinated chicken plus the marinade in the pan. (Put the remaining marinated chicken back in the refrigerator, well covered, for the next recipe.) Cook gently for about 3 minutes, then add the frozen spinach. Stir and cook slowly until fully defrosted and well combined, and the chicken is cooked through, about 5 minutes.

Warm up the chapatis in a low oven or in a dry frying pan.

Serve the curry on fluffy white rice with a dollop of raita and the warm chapatis.

2 FOR 1

BUY 2 CHICKEN BREASTS, MARINATE IN THE FIRST RECIPE, AND USE THE LEFTOVERS IN THE NEXT RECIPE.

CHICKEN TIKKA KABOBS

Leftover marinated chicken from recipe on page 18
½ red onion, thinly sliced
Handful of cherry tomatoes, halved
1 naan bread or wrap (garlic- and/or herb-flavored is the best)
1 to 2 Tbsp plain yogurt
Sea salt and freshly ground black pepper
1 to 2 metal skewers

Preheat the broiler.

Thread the chicken pieces onto 1 to 2 metal skewers, shaping the pieces in such a way that they are all roughly the same size on the skewer. Place the skewer under the broiler and cook for 10 to 15 minutes, turning every now and then to get an even cook. Charring is good, so don't worry about that.

Meanwhile, make a quick salad from the red onion and cherry tomatoes and season with salt and pepper. Stick the naan bread or wrap under the hot broiler to warm through.

When the chicken is cooked through, remove from the broiler (careful—the skewer will be hot!). Slide the chicken from the skewer onto the warmed naan bread or wrap, drizzle over some streaks of yogurt, and eat with the salad.

GRIDDLED CHICKEN BREAST
WITH COUSCOUS AND BLACK OLIVES

Flattened griddled chicken is something I eat all the time, at least once a week—very simple and healthy. You can transform the leftover chicken breast into something spicy, fruity, and with crunch—an easy but exceptional lunch. My brother was around when I was testing this recipe and he has since stolen it and takes it into work all the time. Success!

2 chicken breasts, removed from
    the refrigerator about 20 minutes
    before cooking
Squeeze of lemon juice
Olive oil, for frying
½ cup [100 g] couscous (I use
    whole wheat)
⅝ to ¾ cup [150 to 180 ml] boiling
    chicken broth
2 tomatoes
Handful of black olives, pitted
Sea salt and freshly ground black
    pepper

2 FOR 1

BUY 2 CHICKEN BREASTS,
COOK THEM IN THE FIRST
RECIPE, AND USE THE
LEFTOVERS IN THE
NEXT RECIPE.

Leaving a good space between them, put the chicken breasts on a piece of plastic wrap on a board or counter. Put a second piece of plastic wrap on top and flatten the chicken by bashing and rolling a rolling pin over it. The pieces should end up being about ¼ in [½ cm] thick. Place the flattened chicken on a plate and squeeze over a good amount of lemon juice, a grind of black pepper, and a drizzle of olive oil over both sides.

Pour the boiling chicken broth over the couscous in a heatproof bowl; the broth should come ⅛ in [¼ cm] above the couscous. Cover with a clean dish towel and set aside.

Heat a griddle pan over high heat until it starts to smoke (make sure your extractor fan is on). Season the chicken with salt and griddle for 2 to 3 minutes each side, or until cooked through. Remove and let rest.

Meanwhile, once the couscous has absorbed all the broth and is nice and fluffy, add a drizzle of olive oil and some black pepper (the chicken broth will probably be salty enough), and run a fork through it.

Slice the tomatoes. Plate up half the couscous and top with tomatoes and black olives. Add 1 griddled chicken breast and squeeze over a bit more lemon. Let the remaining chicken breast and couscous cool, then cover and refrigerate until ready to use in the next recipe.

MOROCCAN CHICKEN SALAD

1 tsp rose harissa paste
Leftover cooked couscous from
    recipe above
Handful of shelled pistachios,
    chopped
1 leftover cooked chicken breast
    from recipe above
1 orange, cut into segments

Using a fork, mix the harissa into the couscous. Add the pistachios and mix again. Cut the chicken into strips.

Put the couscous in a bowl and top with the chicken and orange.

CHICKEN LIVER WRAP

I find that liver is sadly underrated. It's cheap, healthy, and has a really rich, deep savoriness. You can do both of these dishes at the same time; once the liver is cooked, eat your wrap while warm and then dive straight into the pâté recipe. When I conjured up this pâté in my head, I had no idea if it would work. Turns out it's a delicious alternative to the classic. It makes a lot of pâté, so you should have plenty for the next few days. You can always pot it up into smaller containers and freeze it for another time.

1 pack of chicken livers
  [14 oz/400 g]
Splash of peanut oil
2 small red onions, thinly sliced
Pinch of sea salt
2 garlic cloves, crushed
½-in [1-cm] piece of ginger, peeled
  and grated
1 Tbsp tikka masala paste
  (I use Patak's)
3 heaping Tbsp [50 ml] water
1 wrap
1 to 2 Tbsp plain yogurt
2-in [5-cm] piece of cucumber, cut into
  thin sticks
A few lettuce leaves

2 FOR 1

BUY 14 OZ [400 G] CHICKEN LIVERS, COOK THEM IN THE FIRST RECIPE, AND USE THE LEFTOVERS IN THE NEXT RECIPE.

Prep the chicken livers by slicing them into thirds and removing any white sinew.

Heat the peanut oil in a large saucepan over low heat, then add the red onions and salt. Cook until soft and golden brown. Add the garlic and ginger, cook for 1 minute, then add the curry paste and cook, stirring regularly, for another 2 minutes. Pour in the water and cook until it has almost all evaporated.

Turn up the heat slightly and add the livers. Stir to coat them in the curry mix and cook, turning regularly, until they are cooked through. Take care in making sure that the curry paste does not stick to the pan.

Meanwhile, prepare the wrap by spooning on, in a circular motion, the plain yogurt. Arrange about one-quarter of the cooked livers in a line on the wrap. Add the cucumber sticks and lettuce. Roll it up and it's time to eat. Make the next recipe after if you can—it'll just take a few minutes!

CHICKEN LIVER PATE

10½ oz [300 g] leftover
  cooked chicken livers from
  recipe above
About ½ cup [100 g] light
  cream cheese
Squeeze of lemon juice
2 to 3½ Tbsp [25 to 50 g]
  butter, melted
Salt and black pepper

Put the still-warm chicken livers, cream cheese, and lemon juice in a food processor and blitz until quite smooth. Season to taste with salt and pepper. For a smoother pâté, add more cream cheese and lemon.

Spoon the pâté into a bowl, let cool for 5 minutes, then top with melted butter. Once completely cool, refrigerate, and eat within the next few days on crunchy toast.

CHICKEN AND LEEK PASTA

This is slightly healthier than it might sound—but just as delicious! To make it even better for you, choosing light cream cheese cuts down on the fat and the dish works just as well with whole wheat pasta. The second recipe, for frittata, is a wonderful way of using leftover pasta. Serve with a simple arugula and tomato salad and you'll have yourself a hearty, satisfying meal.

2 leeks
2 chicken breasts
Small piece of butter
Splash of white wine or Noilly Prat
    vermouth
3½ to 5¼ oz [100 to 150 g] penne
Olive oil, for frying
1 tsp chopped fresh tarragon
    (optional)
2 Tbsp cream cheese
1 tsp Dijon mustard
2 Tbsp milk
Lemon juice (optional)
Sea salt and freshly ground black
    pepper

Put a large saucepan of cold water, with a dash of salt, onto boil for the pasta. Meanwhile, wash and slice the leeks into ⅜-in [1-cm] thick circles. Cut the chicken breasts into bite-size chunks, about ¾ in [2 cm] big.

While the water is heating up for the pasta, put the butter in a heavy-bottom pan over low heat. Once the butter begins to foam, add the leeks and wine and cover the pan. Cook, stirring regularly, until the leeks have softened.

Put the pasta in the pan of boiling water at this stage and cook it according to the package directions.

While the leeks and pasta cook, heat a little olive oil in a frying pan over high heat, brown the chicken, seasoning with salt and pepper as you do so. Once it has browned, add it to the leeks and continue to cook until the chicken pieces are cooked through. If you're using tarragon, stir it in now.

Prepare the sauce by mixing the cream cheese, mustard, milk, and a grind of pepper. Taste and adjust to your palate.

When everything is cooked, drain the pasta and put it back into the dry saucepan with the chicken and leek mixture and the sauce. Adjust the seasoning, stir, and plate up half of it. Let the rest cool, cover, and refrigerate until ready to use in the next recipe.

Add a little lemon juice, if desired. The pasta is perfect served with some garlic ciabatta and a glass of white wine.

2 FOR 1

BUY 2 CHICKEN BREASTS, COOK THEM IN THE FIRST RECIPE, AND USE THE LEFTOVERS IN THE NEXT RECIPE.

CREAMY PASTA FRITTATA

3 large eggs
Splash of water
10½ to 12¼ oz [300 to 350 g] leftover creamy chicken and leek
  pasta from recipe on page 24
Scant ½ cup [50 g] grated cheddar cheese
Small piece of butter

Preheat the broiler.

Beat the eggs and water together. Add the leftover pasta and the cheese and combine.

Melt the butter in an ovenproof frying pan over low heat, add the egg mixture, and cook very slowly. Once it looks cooked about three-quarters of the way through, remove from the heat and place under the broiler. When it has fully cooked and started to turn golden brown, remove it from the broiler and slide it onto a warmed plate.

BBQ CHICKEN BURGER
WITH SWEET POTATO WEDGES AND ULTIMATE CHOCOLATE MILKSHAKE

For me, this is just the best. Proper American diner-style food. Nothing to apologize for, just pure indulgence. In the delightful pasta dish that follows, chorizo proves itself once again a staple in the world of leftovers—it packs an extraordinary punch every time and certainly perks up this dish.

1 large or 2 small sweet potatoes
¼ tsp hot smoked paprika
½ tsp dried red pepper flakes
½ tsp dried oregano
Olive oil, for roasting
2 chicken breasts
Squeeze of lemon
1 bread bun
Dollop of mayonnaise
1 to 2 lettuce leaves
1 tomato, sliced
Sea salt and freshly ground black
    pepper

BBQ sauce
½ Tbsp brown sauce
1 Tbsp ketchup
¼ tsp hot smoked paprika
2 tsp honey

Milkshake
1¼ cups [300 ml] milk
4 to 6 heaping Tbsp chocolate ice
    cream (Ben and Jerry's Chocolate
    Fudge Brownie is the best!)

Preheat the oven to 425°F [220°C].

Wash the sweet potato and cut it into wedges. Place the wedges in a freezer bag with the paprika, dried red pepper flakes, oregano, some salt and pepper, and 2 tsp olive oil. Seal and give it a good shake to coat the wedges well. Tip onto a baking sheet and roast in the preheated oven for 30 minutes.

Leaving a good space between them, put the chicken breasts on a piece of plastic wrap on a board or counter. Put a second piece of plastic wrap on top and flatten the chicken by bashing and rolling a rolling pin over it. The pieces should end up being about ⅜ in [1 cm] thick. Place the flattened chicken on a plate and squeeze over a good amount of lemon juice, a grind of black pepper, and a drizzle of olive oil over both sides.

Mix the ingredients for the BBQ sauce. Remove the ice cream from the freezer, ready for the milkshake.

When the potato wedges have about 15 minutes left, heat a griddle pan over high heat until it starts to smoke (make sure your extractor fan is on). Season the chicken with salt and griddle for 3 to 4 minutes each side, or until cooked through. Remove and let rest.

For the milkshake, blitz the milk and most of the softened ice cream with a hand blender in a measuring cup (or use a blender). (If you like your milkshake thicker, add more ice cream and less milk.) Add the last scoop of ice cream but only blitz for a second to keep a few lovely chunks. Serve in a large glass.

Cut the burger bun in half through the middle. Spread the mayonnaise over one side, then add the lettuce, one chicken breast, a smear of BBQ sauce, and the tomato. Stack up your potato wedges and enjoy the cooling shake.

2 FOR 1

BUY 2 CHICKEN BREASTS, COOK THEM IN THE FIRST RECIPE, AND USE THE LEFTOVERS IN THE NEXT RECIPE.

CHICKEN AND CHORIZO PASTA BOWL

1¾ oz [50 g] penne
3½ oz [100 g] chorizo
1 leftover cooked chicken breast from recipe
  on page 28
Good drizzle of olive oil
Squeeze of lemon juice
2 tomatoes, quartered
Handful of arugula
Drizzle of balsamic vinegar
Sea salt and freshly ground black pepper
Grated Parmesan, to serve (optional)

Put a large saucepan of cold water, with a dash of salt, onto boil for the penne. Cook the penne according to the package directions.

Meanwhile, slice the chorizo and chicken into ⅜-in [1-cm] thick strips (or dice the chorizo if desired). Heat the olive oil in a frying pan over medium-low heat, then fry the chorizo until golden brown. Add the chicken, reduce the heat, and cook until piping hot.

Drain the pasta and add it to the frying pan. Add the lemon juice, a little more oil, if you feel it needs it, and some salt and pepper to taste. Tip into a large bowl and top with the tomatoes, arugula, and balsamic vinegar. Add some grated Parmesan, if desired.

BAKED LEMON CHICKEN LEGS

Chicken legs done this way make for a harmonious, rounded dish, allowing loads of flavor to be absorbed into the components. It also means less cleaning up! Watching *The Sopranos* always made me hungry and this chicken eggplant parmigiana recipe is something Tony would be proud of!

Olive oil, for frying
2 chicken legs
8¾ oz [250 g] new potatoes
1 lemon
6 garlic cloves, peeled
Handful of fresh thyme
⅝ cup [150 ml] chicken broth or white wine
Squeeze of honey
Sea salt and freshly ground black pepper

Preheat the oven to 350°F [180°C].

Heat a dash of olive oil in a Dutch oven over high heat. Season the chicken legs well with salt and pepper, then brown them all over in the Dutch oven. Remove the dish from the heat and put the chicken legs onto a plate.

Slice the new potatoes into quarters, or sixths for larger ones. Cut the lemon into segments, discarding the peel and bitter white pith. Add to the Dutch oven with the potatoes, garlic, thyme, broth, and honey. Season with salt and pepper and pop the chicken legs back into the dish.

Put the lid on the dish and bake in the preheated oven for 40 minutes. Now remove the lid and cook for another 10 minutes, or until the chicken and potatoes are cooked through. Let the chicken rest for a few minutes. Serve 1 chicken leg in a bowl with the potatoes, garlic, and chicken liquor from the dish. Let the other chicken leg cool, then cover and refrigerate until ready to use in the next recipe.

2 FOR 1

BUY 2 CHICKEN LEGS, COOK BOTH IN THE FIRST RECIPE, AND USE THE LEFTOVERS IN THE NEXT RECIPE.

EGGPLANT CHICKEN PARMIGIANA

Olive oil, for frying
2 garlic cloves, crushed
14-oz [400-g] can chopped tomatoes
½ tsp sugar
1 medium eggplant
1 leftover cooked chicken leg from recipe left
5¼ oz [150 g] cooking mozzarella
Small handful of fresh basil leaves, torn
Sea salt and freshly ground black pepper

Preheat the oven to 375°F [190°C].

Heat a glug of olive oil in a saucepan over low heat and sweat the garlic for a couple of minutes. Add the chopped tomatoes and season with the sugar and some salt and pepper. Cook over low heat, stirring regularly, for at least 10 minutes.

Slice the eggplant into ⅜-in [1-cm] thick circles. Season with salt and pepper and brush with a little olive oil. Heat a griddle pan over high heat and once smoking, griddle the eggplant for 1 minute each side, or until lightly charred.

Tear the chicken off the bone and into bite-size chunks and thinly slice the mozzarella.

Layer the tomato sauce, eggplant, torn basil, chicken, and mozzarella in an ovenproof dish. Bake in the preheated oven for 30 minutes. Serve with crunchy ciabatta, a fresh side salad, and a glass of red.

ROAST CHICKEN

A roast is a very personal thing so I'm leaving the accompanying veg up to you ... I suggest carrots, parsnips, endive, or some simple steamed broccoli—but you choose! The large quantities of potatoes are needed so that you can use half for the potato cakes in the next few days. Because they've already been roasted, the potatoes and chicken are bursting with flavor, making the cakes supertasty. Don't skimp on the tarragon, as it takes these potato cakes to a whole new level. You'll also find here two other favorites—a selection of incredible sandwiches and a hearty chicken soup which makes enough for a few helpings. I did try to choose just one ultimate sandwich but I couldn't. So I've given you a few of the options I love.

1 large chicken [to serve 3 to 4, about 2½ lb/1.2 kg]
Olive oil, for frying
Juice of ½ lemon
Fresh herbs, such as rosemary, thyme, or sage (optional)
4 to 5 slices of lean bacon (optional)
15¾ oz [450 g] potatoes, quartered and parboiled
Goose or duck fat, for frying (optional)
2 cups [500 ml] chicken broth
Sea salt and freshly ground black pepper

Preheat the oven to 350°F [180°C]. Weigh the chicken and work out the cooking time you need—20 minutes per 15¾ oz [450 g], plus an extra 20 minutes.

Sit the chicken in a large roasting tray. Drizzle some olive oil and the lemon juice over the bird. Add any herbs you want. Season with salt and pepper. Lay the slices of bacon over, too, if desired. Roast the chicken in the preheated oven for the period of time you worked out earlier. With 50 minutes to go, place the parboiled potatoes around the chicken in the tray with a drizzle of olive oil or spoonful of goose or duck fat, and season well with salt and pepper. Baste the chicken every 20 minutes, or so and turn the potatoes.

To check if the chicken is properly cooked: the leg should be loose, the juices run clear, and the meat should be white. Remove the bird and potatoes from the tray and let rest in a warm place. Place the tray on the stove and add the broth. Scrape the bottom of the pan to get all the flavorsome bits involved. Let bubble and boil for a few minutes, then decant into a gravy pitcher. Serve it all up! Let the leftover chicken (including the carcass) and potatoes cool, cover, and refrigerate until ready to use in the following recipes. Set aside any leftover gravy, too, for the chicken soup later on.

4 FOR 1

BUY A WHOLE CHICKEN, COOK IT IN THE FIRST RECIPE, AND USE THE LEFTOVERS IN THE FOLLOWING RECIPES.

CHICKEN SANDWICHES

CLASSIC bread, leftover roast chicken, salt and black pepper, mayonnaise, lettuce, tomato

BBQ bread roll, leftover roast chicken, BBQ sauce, chorizo, cheese

PESTO toasted bread, pesto, mozzarella, cherry tomatoes, leftover roast chicken

TZATZIKI wrap, feta, tomato, tzatziki, leftover roast chicken, radishes, pickled chiles

CORONATION mayonnaise, lemon juice, curry powder, mango chutney, leftover roast chicken

CHICKEN AND TARRAGON POTATO CAKES

3½ oz [100 g] leftover leg and thigh
chicken meat from recipe on
page 35
7 oz [200 g] leftover roast potatoes
from recipe on page 35
(or mashed potato)
Handful of fresh tarragon, minced
A little all-purpose flour
Small piece of butter
Sea salt and freshly ground black
pepper

Finely dice the chicken meat. Briefly blitz the leftover roast potatoes using a hand blender or food processor until quite smooth. Mix the chicken and potato together with the tarragon and some salt and pepper.

Put some flour on your hands and shape the mixture into 2 patties. Add a dusting of flour on the outside of the patties.

Melt the butter in a frying pan over low heat. Once it foams, add the patties and cook for a couple of minutes each side, or until golden brown. Serve with a salad of tomatoes, arugula, and balsamic dressing.

CHICKEN SOUP

1 leftover chicken carcass from
    recipe on page 35
8 cups [2 L] water
2 celery stalks
1 onion, peeled and cut into quarters
Handful of fresh parsley sprigs,
    separated into stalks and
    chopped leaves
1⅔ cups [400 ml] leftover gravy
    from recipe on page 35
Scant 1 cup [100 g] macaroni
Any leftover cooked chicken from
    recipe on page 35, shredded
Veg of your choice, such as frozen
    peas, fava beans, baby carrots,
    and/or sliced zucchini

Put the chicken carcass, water, celery, onion, and parsley stalks in a large saucepan or stockpot. Cover and bring to a boil. Cook for 50 minutes.

Drain the broth through a colander into separate saucepan. Add the gravy and bring to a boil. Once boiling, add the macaroni and cook until 3 minutes before the macaroni ought to be cooked according to the package directions. At that moment, add the leftover chicken and any of your chosen veg.

Ladle into a bowl and sprinkle the chopped parsley leaves over the top. Let the leftover soup cool, then cover and refrigerate to enjoy another day.

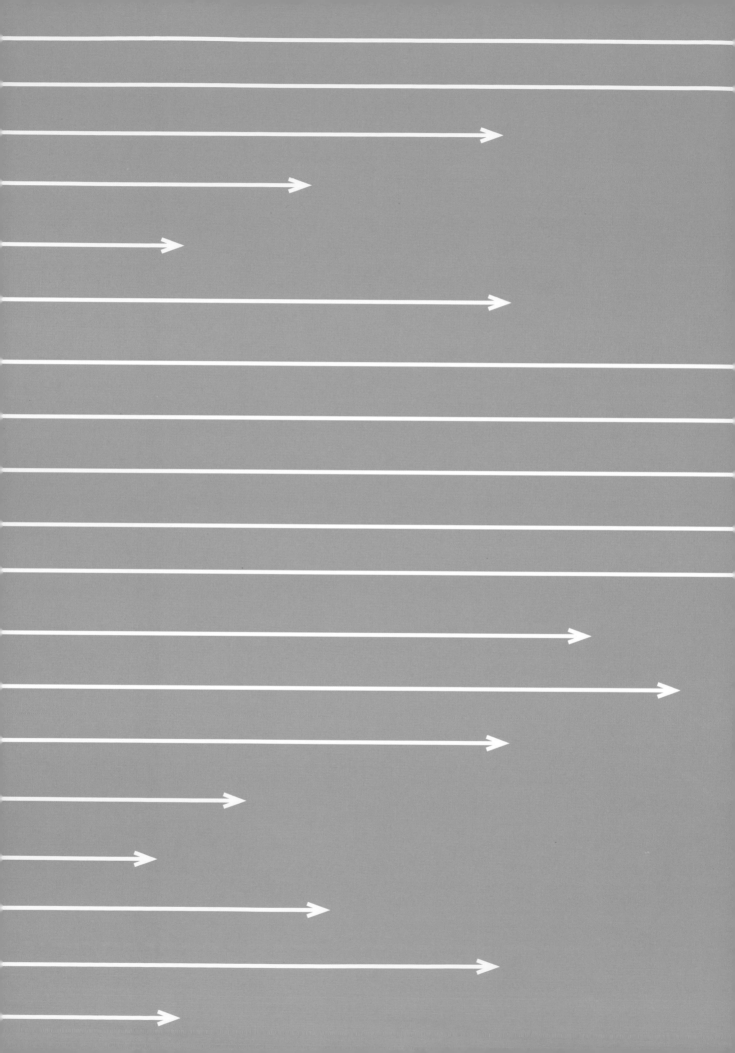

COOK DUCK

FIVE-SPICE DUCK LEGS
WITH CHILI SWEET POTATO MASH

Duck legs are as cheap as duck gets, but actually they are the most succulent and deeply flavorsome. The sweet potato mash is spiked with chili and makes a much better accompaniment than the usual old mashed potatoes. The easy soy and honey sauce really hits the spot. For the second recipe, shred the leftover duck and enjoy it in these classic Chinese lettuce wraps.

2 duck legs
1 tsp coarse sea salt
1 tsp five-spice powder
10½ oz [300 g] sweet potato
Small splash of toasted sesame oil
1¼-in [3-cm] piece of ginger, peeled and grated
1 to 2 pinches dried red pepper flakes or minced fresh chile
2 tsp soy sauce
Fresh cilantro, torn (optional)

Honey and soy sauce
4 Tbsp rice wine
2 Tbsp water
2 tsp dark soy sauce
1 tsp honey

Preheat the oven to 400°F [200°C].

Place the duck legs in a roasting tray and prick them all over with a fork. Rub the skin with the sea salt and five-spice powder. Cook for 1 hour 20 minutes, draining the fat off as you go (roughly every 20 to 30 minutes).

Put a saucepan of water onto boil. Peel and slice the sweet potato into ⅜-in [1-cm] chunks and boil in the pan of water for 7 minutes, or until cooked. Mash. Meanwhile, heat the sesame oil in a small pan over low heat, then sweat the ginger and red pepper flakes or chili for a few minutes. Add a little water if it sticks. Add to the mashed potato with the soy sauce and beat together with a wooden spoon. Top or mix through with cilantro, if desired.

Prepare the honey and soy sauce by mixing the ingredients together in a saucepan, bringing to a boil, and then simmering for 1 minute.

Once the duck has had its time in the oven, remove, and let it rest for a few minutes. Plate up by creating a pile of the mash, putting one of the duck legs on top, and covering with the sauce. Let the other duck leg cool, cover, and refrigerate it until ready to use in the next recipe.

LETTUCE WRAPS WITH SHREDDED DUCK AND HOISIN SAUCE

1 leftover cooked duck leg from recipe above
¼ cucumber
1 scallion
3 to 4 crisp leaves of iceberg lettuce
2 to 3 Tbsp hoisin sauce

Shred the duck leg. Cut the cucumber into thin sticks and finely shred the scallion. Make up the wraps as you would for crispy duck pancakes: lettuce, a spoon of hoisin, cucumber, scallion, and shredded duck.

2 FOR 1

BUY 2 DUCK LEGS, COOK
THEM IN THE FIRST RECIPE,
AND USE THE LEFTOVERS IN
THE NEXT RECIPE.

DUCK LEGS IN PLUM SAUCE
WITH ASIAN GREENS

The duck legs in the first recipe just look after themselves in the oven, so you can focus on getting the tasty Asian greens just right. Remember this way of cooking these greens—they can be teamed up with all sorts of future supper dishes that are crying out for great veg! The leftover duck leg is cleverly reinvented to make a mighty ragu, packed with punch, that can be served with pasta or polenta.

2 duck legs
Good pinch of sea salt
2 Tbsp plum sauce
2 scallions
1¼-in [3-cm] piece of ginger, peeled
2 garlic cloves
1 chile
1 large pak choi
Toasted sesame oil, for frying
1 Tbsp dark soy sauce
1 Tbsp oyster sauce
Squeeze of lime juice

Preheat the oven to 400°F [200°C].

Place the duck legs in a roasting tray and prick them all over with a fork. Rub the skin with the salt and spoon the plum sauce over them. Cook for 1 hour, draining the fat off occasionally if a lot of it runs off. Then reduce the oven temperature to 350°F [180°C] and continue to cook the duck for 10 minutes, basting it well with the plum sauce.

Take the duck out of the oven and let it rest for a few minutes. Top with more plum sauce, if desired.

Meanwhile, prep the fresh ingredients. Slice the scallions into ⅜-in [1-cm] circles; cut the ginger into thin sticks; crush the garlic; slice the chile into thin rings; and chop the pak choi into bite-size chunks.

Heat a good drizzle of sesame oil in a wok over low heat and add the scallions, ginger, and garlic. Stir-fry for 2 to 3 minutes, then add the chile, and continue to cook for a minute. Add the pak choi and soy and oyster sauces. Stir-fry for a couple of minutes until the pak choi begins to wilt.

Plate up one of the duck legs with the Asian greens and serve with noodles, if desired. Let the other duck leg cool, cover, and refrigerate it until ready to use in the next recipe.

2 FOR 1

BUY 2 DUCK LEGS, COOK THEM IN THE FIRST RECIPE, AND USE THE LEFTOVERS IN THE NEXT RECIPE.

DUCK RAGU

3 garlic cloves
1 carrot, peeled
2 celery stalks
Olive oil, for frying
⅝ cup [150 ml] red wine
1 leftover cooked duck leg from recipe left
14-oz [400-g] can chopped tomatoes
1 tsp sugar
2 rosemary sprigs
About 3½ oz [100 g] pasta of your choice
Sea salt and freshly ground black pepper
Grated Parmesan, to serve

Crush the garlic, and finely dice the carrot and celery. Heat a good glug of olive oil in a heavy-bottom saucepan over low heat and sweat the garlic, carrot, and celery for 5 minutes.

Add the red wine and cook until it has reduced down by about half, about 5 minutes.

Meanwhile, take the leftover cooked duck leg and remove the meat from the bone in bite-size chunks. Keep the bone.

Add the canned tomatoes, sugar, rosemary, and bone to the pan and simmer slowly for 10 minutes, stirring regularly. You will want to put a pan of water on for the pasta at this point; start to cook it at the right moment and cook it according to the package directions.

Add the duck to the ragu pan and taste for seasoning. Heat up gently until the duck is piping hot.

Remove the duck bone and sprigs of rosemary. Stir the ragu through the pasta, plate up, and serve with a liberal grating of Parmesan.

SMOKY DUCK BREAST
WITH GRIDDLED ASPARAGUS

Using smoked salt is a great way of imparting a further level of flavor to your duck; it works just as well with steak. Cooking duck this way will render down all of the fat to give you a crisp but fairly lean breast—this then works beautifully in a light and fresh Vietnamese salad that I found on my travels.

2 duck breasts
Smoked sea salt
Small bunch of asparagus
Olive oil, for frying
1 lemon
*Sea salt and freshly ground black
    pepper*

Preheat the oven to 400°F [200°C].

Heat a dry nonstick frying pan over medium heat. Score the duck breasts with a sharp knife with a crisscross pattern and season generously with the smoked sea salt and some pepper. Season the underside of the breast a little, too.

Place the duck breasts, skin side down, into the hot frying pan and cook for about 3 minutes until golden and crisp. Turn them over and sear the other side of the breasts quickly before pouring away the fat. Transfer the duck to an ovenproof dish and roast in the oven for 6 to 8 minutes depending on the thickness of the duck and how pink you like it. Remove from the oven and let rest.

Meanwhile, coat the asparagus in olive oil and a good squeeze of lemon juice, and season with salt and pepper. Heat a griddle pan over high heat, then add the asparagus and cook for 1 to 2 minutes per side until charred and cooked. Remove from the pan and squeeze over a little more lemon juice.

Slice one duck breast and plate up the asparagus and your chosen side dish, such as mashed cannellini beans (see page 120) or pan-fried potatoes. Let the other duck breast cool, then cover and refrigerate until ready for the next recipe.

2 FOR 1

BUY 2 DUCK BREASTS, COOK THEM IN THE FIRST RECIPE, AND USE THE LEFTOVERS IN THE NEXT RECIPE.

VIETNAMESE DUCK SALAD

1 leftover cooked duck breast from recipe left
1 small romaine lettuce
1 small mango
Handful of radishes
Handful of fresh mint, torn
Handful of fresh cilantro, torn

Dressing
1 Tbsp sweet chili sauce
1 Tbsp fish sauce
1 Tbsp rice wine vinegar
½ Tbsp lime juice

Make the dressing by combining all the ingredients in a bowl.

Cut the cooked duck breast into thin slices. Tear the lettuce into bite-size pieces. Peel and seed the mango and cut the flesh into thin sticks. Thinly slice the radishes. Put the lettuce into a bowl and coat in the dressing. Top with the mango, radishes, duck slices, and torn herbs.

ROAST DUCK

Here we have duck three ways, so you can really make the most of a whole duck, which might not be a meat you would normally consider cooking. The whole roast duck in the first instance is a hearty, warming feast; the borek is a tasty Greek temptation made with phyllo dough and good for two servings. It can be made as individual packages, or as one pie. Later on in the week, make the rolls in double-quick time—they are irresistible ...

1 large duck
Sea salt
Red Wine Gravy (see page 92)

Preheat the oven to 425°F [220°C].

Stab the duck all over with a fork. Rub some sea salt all over the skin. Put it on a rack in a roasting tray and place in the oven.

After 20 minutes of roasting, reduce the oven temperature to 375°F [190°C]. Continue to roast until the skin is crispy, the bird is tender, and the juices run clear when you pierce the flesh with a sharp knife. This will take about 1 hour 30 minutes to 2 hours.

When the duck is cooked, the fat will have run off into the tray—save it for cooking with another time! It's the best friend a roast potato ever had. Let the duck rest for a few minutes.

Carve the duck and set both legs aside for the following recipes. Serve the duck breast meat with the Red Wine Gravy poured over it. Eat with lightly sautéed, buttered cabbage, and your choice of potatoes.

3 FOR 1

BUY A WHOLE DUCK, COOK IT IN THE FIRST RECIPE, AND USE THE LEFTOVERS IN THE FOLLOWING RECIPES.

DUCK, FETA, AND SPINACH PHYLLO PIE

About 3½ Tbsp [50 g] butter
4¼ oz [125 g] fresh spinach
1 leftover roasted duck leg from
  recipe on page 49
1¾ oz [50 g] feta
1 tsp chopped fresh mint
¼ to ½ tsp grated nutmeg
½ egg, lightly beaten
4 sheets of phyllo dough
Freshly ground black pepper

Melt ½ Tbsp butter in a saucepan. Once foaming, add the spinach and cook for a few minutes until wilted. Transfer to a bowl and let cool for 5 minutes.

Meanwhile, take the duck leg, discard the skin, and shred the meat into small bite-size pieces. Crumble the feta.

Put the spinach in a clean dish towel and wring out the excess moisture from the spinach. Place it back in the bowl with the feta, duck, mint, nutmeg, egg, and a grind of black pepper. Mix and let cool further.

Preheat the oven to 375°F [190°C].

Melt the remaining butter.

To make little individual packages, or borek
Lay the phyllo dough sheets out on a board and cut them into quarters. Take one rectangle and keep the others covered with a dish towel to prevent them from drying out. Brush melted butter liberally over the rectangle. Place a second one on top, brush with butter, add a third rectangle, brush with butter, and finally top with a fourth rectangle (but do not brush with butter). Spoon the filling diagonally along the middle of the pile of phyllo dough sheets. Now brush the edges with butter and fold over the pastry to form a triangle. Place on a greased baking sheet. Repeat with the remaining pieces of phyllo—buttering, stacking, filling, and folding. Brush melted butter lightly over the top.

To make one big pie
Grease a small pie dish (about 7 in/18 cm in diameter and 1¼ in/3 cm deep). Lay the phyllo dough sheets out on a board and brush melted butter liberally over 3 of them. Stack them up, then lay them inside the pie dish. Let the edges spill over the sides. Spoon the filling in the middle, then fold the phyllo edges over toward the middle, over the filling. Place the last sheet of phyllo over the top to cover the pie completely.

Cook the little borek or big pie in the preheated oven for about 15 to 18 minutes, or until the pastry is well browned.

BIG COOK
LEFTOVERS

BBQ DUCK ROLLS
WITH HOT SAUCE

*1 leftover roasted duck leg from
   recipe on page 49*
BBQ Sauce (see page 28)
1 bread bun
Dollop of mayonnaise
1 tomato, sliced
1 to 2 salad leaves
Hot sauce (optional)

Pull the duck from the bone and shred it. Mix it with enough BBQ sauce to taste. Layer up your bun with the mayonnaise, salad leaves, duck, tomato, and some hot sauce to fire it up.

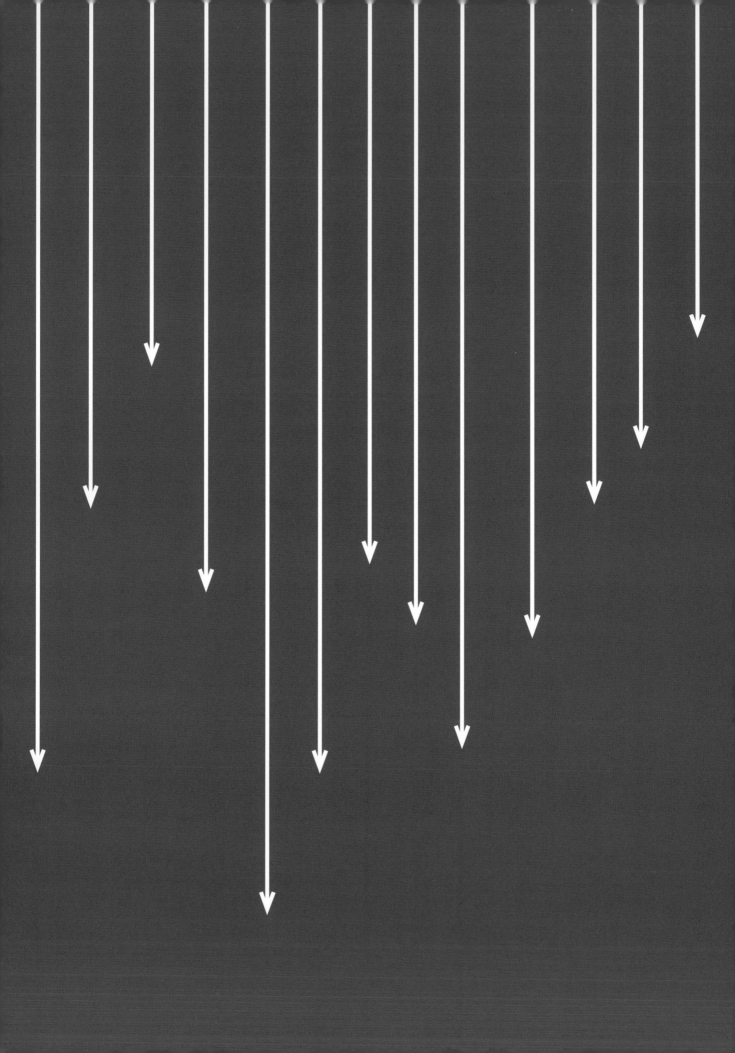

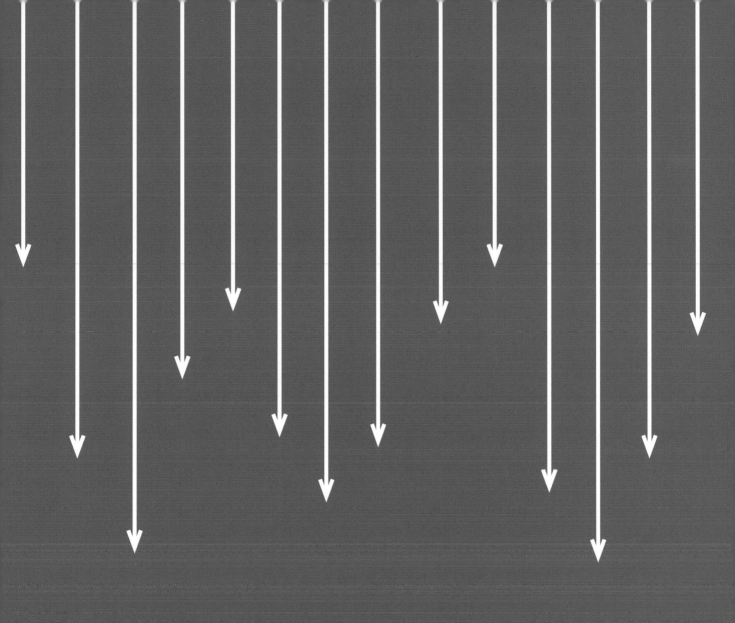

COOK

BEEF

2 FOR 1

BUY 7 OZ [200 G] TOP ROUND STEAK AND COOK HALF IN EACH RECIPE.

PHILLY CHEESESTEAK SANDWICH

This couple starts with a brilliant top round steak. Thinly sliced, it can be as tender as the finest fillet but actually with more flavor. So the Philly sandwich is a real self-indulgent treat—it's the cheese that does it! Its partner recipe, opposite, provides some lighter relief, using easy sweet-roasted peppers from a jar. Together they'll make your steak go further than you could ever think possible. Magic!

1 onion
Butter, for frying
Scant ¼ cup [50 g] cream cheese
Scant ½ cup [50 g] grated extra sharp cheddar cheese
3½ oz [100 g] top round steak
Squeeze of lemon juice
Glug of olive oil
1 sandwich-size ciabatta or sub
Sea salt and freshly ground black pepper

Thinly slice the onion. Add a little piece of butter to a frying pan over low heat and once it's foaming, add the onion and a pinch of salt, and fry until soft and golden brown, 5 to 8 minutes.

Meanwhile, combine the cream cheese and cheddar in a saucepan. Cook over low heat until it becomes a thick and creamy cheese sauce.

Heat a griddle pan until it is smoking (make sure your extractor fan is on). Trim any fat off the steak and slice it across the grain into very thin strips. Put in a bowl with the lemon juice, olive oil, and some salt and pepper just before it hits the pan and stir. Cook in the smoking-hot pan for about 10 seconds each side. Remove from the pan and let rest.

Cut the ciabatta or sub in half through the middle. Arrange the onion on the bottom, the steak in the middle, and the cheese sauce on top. Devour.

STEAK AND ROASTED PEPPER SALAD

3½ oz [100 g] top round steak
Squeeze of lemon juice
Glug of olive oil
Couple of slices of nice bread
   (e.g. ciabatta)
Handful of mixed salad greens
2 roasted red bell peppers from a jar,
   drained
Horseradish sauce
Sea salt and freshly ground black
   pepper

Dressing
1 Tbsp olive oil
1 tsp white wine vinegar
¼ tsp Dijon mustard
Small pinch of sugar
Pinch of minced fresh tarragon

Combine the ingredients for the dressing and give it a good stir.

Heat a griddle pan until it is smoking (make sure your extractor fan is on). Trim any fat off the steak and slice it across the grain into very thin strips. Put it in a bowl with the lemon juice, olive oil, and some salt and pepper just before it hits the pan and give it a good stir. Cook in the smoking-hot pan for about 20 seconds each side, or until it gets a good color. Remove from the pan and let rest. Add the bread to the hot pan and griddle for a minute each side, or until it has a good color.

Toss the salad in the dressing and plate up. Thinly slice the peppers and add to the salad with the steak. Smother the toasts in your preferred amount of horseradish sauce.

BEEF AND ALE PIE

A pair of bar classics. The pie takes under an hour (which is superspeedy for a pie with such depth of flavor) and anything left over, with the addition of cabbage and potato, transforms into gutsy bubble-and-squeak cakes. They're easy to double up if you have enough leftover stew.

10½ oz [300 g] top round steak
Olive oil, for frying
1 large onion, finely diced
5¼ oz [150 g] cremini mushrooms, quartered
Handful of fresh thyme, stalks removed
About ⅝ cup [150 ml] beef broth, plus extra if required
⅝ cup [150 ml] ale
½ Tbsp all-purpose flour
Small piece of butter
Sea salt and freshly ground black pepper
About 3½ oz [100 g] ready-made puff pastry

Trim any fat off the steak and cut it into 2-in [5-cm] chunks. Put a heavy-bottom saucepan or Dutch oven over medium heat. Season the beef all over with salt and pepper and coat it lightly in olive oil. Once the pan has some heat, stick in the beef and quickly seal. Once browned, remove it from the pan and set it aside.

Adjust the heat under the pan to low and add the butter. Once it is foaming, add the onion and a pinch of salt. Fry until soft and golden brown, about 5 to 8 minutes, stirring regularly. Now add the mushrooms and cook for another 2 minutes. Then add the broth and the ale and slowly sprinkle in the flour while stirring to avoid lumps. Bring to a boil, then add the beef. Simmer, uncovered, for 45 minutes, or until the beef is tender. Add more broth if the sauce becomes a little too thick.

Meanwhile, preheat the oven to 425°F [220°C]. Using a rolling pin, roll out the pastry on a floured board to a square 4 in [10 cm] wide and ⅜ in [1 cm] thick. Place on a greased baking sheet and when the beef as just 10 minutes to go, stick the pastry in the preheated oven. Cook for 10 minutes, or until golden brown.

Ladle three-quarters of the beef into a bowl and top with the golden pastry hat. Let the remaining beef cool, then cover and refrigerate until ready to use in the next recipe.

2 FOR 1

BUY 10½ OZ (300 G) TOP ROUND STEAK, COOK IN THE FIRST RECIPE, AND USE THE LEFTOVERS IN THE NEXT.

BUBBLE-AND-SQUEAK CAKES

1 heaping Tbsp leftover beef stew from recipe on page 58
1¾ oz [50 g] cabbage, shredded and cooked
Scant ⅔ cup [150 g] mashed potato (use leftovers from another meal,
*   or make it from scratch following page 72)*
1 to 2 Tbsp all-purpose flour, seasoned with salt and pepper
Small piece of butter
Drizzle of olive oil
Sea salt and freshly ground black pepper

Chop the bits in the leftover stew into smaller pieces. Combine with the cabbage and mashed potato and season with salt and pepper. Form into a patty and coat them in the seasoned flour.

Heat the butter and olive oil in a saucepan over medium-low heat. Add the patty and cook for 3 minutes each side, or until golden brown and piping hot inside. Serve with a fresh salad.

GINGER BEEF BURGER
WITH ASIAN SLAW

Ground beef is cheap, so go for the best you can find; and 20 percent fat content will have superior flavor. This burger is inspired by one of my favorite varieties of dim sum—ginger beef balls—and the accompanying slaw adds a real zesty punch. As for the meatballs, their accompanying tomato sauce is a pure Italian beauty that you're sure to fall in love with.

1 Tbsp mayonnaise
Small handful of fresh
*   cilantro, minced*
Olive oil, for frying
1 burger bun
1 to 2 leaves of iceberg lettuce
1 wedge of lime (optional)

Slaw
¼ white cabbage, root removed
1 carrot, peeled
¾ Tbsp lime juice
1 tsp Chinese rice vinegar
1 Tbsp light soy sauce
2 tsp grated fresh ginger
2 tsp sugar
2 heaping Tbsp mayonnaise

Burger
7 oz [200 g] ground beef
2 tsp grated fresh ginger
⅛ cup [25 g] grated apple
¼ cup [25 g] bread crumbs, plus
*   more if needed*
Small handful of fresh
*   cilantro, minced*
Grated zest of ½ lemon
Sea salt and freshly ground
*   black pepper*

Preheat the oven to 350°F [180°C].

For the slaw, cut the cabbage and carrot into very thin strips using a food processor and shredding attachment, or manually with a knife or grater. Mix together the lime juice, vinegar, soy sauce, ginger, and sugar in one bowl. Put the mayonnaise in a separate bowl and stir in the lime mixture gradually to prevent the mayonnaise from separating. Combine at least 2 Tbsp with the shredded cabbage and carrot, but you can add more if desired.

Combine the ingredients for the burger, season with salt and pepper, and shape into a patty. If it seems a little too wet, add some more bread crumbs. Refrigerate for 5 minutes. Meanwhile, mix together the mayonnaise and cilantro for the filling.

Add a little oil to an ovenproof frying pan over medium heat. Add the patty and cook for a minute or so on each side until golden brown. Transfer to the oven and cook for another 5 to 7 minutes depending on how well done you like it. In the meantime, halve your burger bun and toast it if you like. Spread cilantro mayonnaise over one half and add the lettuce. Once the burger has cooked, let it rest for a few minutes and then place it on the lettuce. Serve with the slaw and a wedge of lime, if desired.

2 FOR 1

BUY 14 OZ [400 G] GROUND BEEF AND USE HALF IN EACH RECIPE.

SPAGHETTI AND MEATBALLS

3½ oz [100 g] spaghetti
Olive oil, for frying
Grated Parmesan, to serve
2 to 3 Tbsp all-purpose flour, seasoned with salt and pepper
Sea salt and freshly ground black pepper

Meatballs
7 oz [200 g] ground beef
Scant ¼ cup [25 g] bread crumbs
1 to 2 garlic cloves
2 tsp dried oregano
Grated zest of ½ lemon
½ to 1 egg, lightly beaten

Tomato sauce
2 garlic cloves, crushed
14-oz [400-g] can chopped tomatoes
1 tsp sugar

Combine the ingredients for the meatballs, adding the whole beaten egg if you feel the mixture is too dry with just half. Season with salt and pepper. Shape into meatballs, roll in the seasoned flour, and set aside as you make the tomato sauce. Heat a glug of oil in a saucepan, then add the garlic and sweat it for a bit. Add the tomatoes, sugar, salt, and pepper and simmer gently for at least 10 minutes.

Cook your pasta according to the package directions. Heat another glug of oil in a frying pan and brown the meatballs over medium heat until cooked through, or add to the simmering tomato sauce for 3 to 5 minutes depending on size.

Pile the sauce and meatballs onto the spaghetti and garnish with Parmesan. If you have any leftover tomato sauce, use it another night or freeze it.

MISO STEAK AND CHILI SWEET POTATO WEDGES

Two more great ways with a top round steak. For the first, the miso adds an exotic sweet saltiness and for the second, the chipotle paste brings a fiery depth that's really exciting and brings the steak to life.

8¾ oz [250 g] top round steak
2 tsp brown miso paste
2 tsp rice wine
2 tsp lemon juice
1 large garlic clove, crushed
Olive oil, for marinating and roasting
1 large sweet potato
1 to 2 tsp dried red pepper flakes
Sea salt and freshly ground black
    pepper

2 FOR 1

BUY 8¾ OZ [250 G] TOP ROUND STEAK, COOK IT IN THE FIRST RECIPE, AND USE THE LEFTOVERS IN THE NEXT RECIPE.

Preheat the oven to 350°F [180°C].

Trim any fat off the steak and cut it across the grain into ⅛-in [¼-cm] thick slices. Combine the miso paste, rice wine, lemon juice, garlic, and a drizzle of olive oil. Add the steak, mix, and let marinate while you prepare the rest of the ingredients.

Wash the sweet potato and cut it into wedges. Coat in olive oil and season with the red pepper flakes and a good amount of salt and pepper. Place on a baking sheet and roast in the preheated oven, turning once, for 20 to 30 minutes, or until golden brown.

When the wedges are nearly ready, stick a griddle pan over high heat (make sure your extractor fan is on). Once smoking, add the steak in batches so as not to overcrowd the pan. Cook for 20 seconds each side, or until it has a good color. Do not overcook! Remove from the pan and let rest in a warm place. Cook the remaining steak in the same way.

To serve, pile about three-fifths of the steak high in the middle on a plate and surround with wonderful wedges. Add a few green leaves, if desired. Let the remaining steak cool, then cover and refrigerate until ready to use in the next recipe.

CHIPOTLE STEAK AND CHEESE QUESADILLAS

3½ oz [100 g] leftover cooked
    top round steak from
    recipe above
2 to 3 tsp chipotle paste
2 tortillas (I use seeded
    whole wheat)
3 Tbsp refried beans
Scant ½ cup [50 g] grated
    sharp cheddar cheese
Handful of fresh cilantro,
    torn
Guacamole, to serve
Sour cream, to serve

Combine the leftover steak in a bowl with the chipotle paste. Let sit for a few minutes while you prepare the rest of the ingredients.

Take 1 tortilla and spread over the refried beans. Spread out the steak over the beans and cover in grated cheddar and torn cilantro. Place the other tortilla on top. Heat a dry frying pan over medium heat. When hot, place the quesadilla in the pan and cook for 1 to 2 minutes each side until golden and crisp and the filling is piping hot. Remove, place on a board, and cut into slices. Serve with dollops of guacamole and sour cream.

BBQ BEEF RIBS

Ribs are a big hunk of meat, deep, and rich—and thrifty! This first recipe is for a lazy Sunday when you just want to overindulge. It takes minimal effort for such a great result. The second recipe, for the BBQ rib sandwich, is a piece of cake ... Ask your butcher to order these ribs in for you. You are looking for 2 ribs, about 7 in [18 cm] long and 3 in [7.5 cm] wide. If you can't get the exact weight or size, don't worry; adjust the cooking time a little to compensate. They are such a good piece of meat ...

3¼ lb [1.5 kg] beef ribs
BBQ Sauce (see page 28)

Dry rub
1½ Tbsp hot smoked paprika
¾ Tbsp sea salt
¾ Tbsp freshly ground black pepper
¾ Tbsp ground cumin
2 tsp chili powder
¾ Tbsp brown sugar
2 tsp cayenne pepper

Preheat the oven to 350 °F [180 °C].

Place the ribs in a roasting tray. Mix the ingredients for the dry rub and rub generously all over the ribs. If you have any left, store it in a jar for another day.

Roast the ribs in the preheated oven for 3 hours, or until the meat falls off the bone and you can use a fork to pull it apart easily. Slather with BBQ Sauce and serve with a light salad or some buttered corn on the cob. Shred the leftover meat off the rib while still warm (it's easier to do this way), then cover and refrigerate until ready to use in the next recipe.

2 FOR 1

BUY 3¼ LB [1.5 KG] BEEF RIBS, COOK THEM IN THE FIRST RECIPE, AND USE THE LEFTOVERS IN THE NEXT RECIPE.

BBQ RIB SANDWICH

Shredded leftover beef from recipe above
BBQ Sauce (see page 28)
2 lettuce leaves
2 slices of tomato
Bread roll

Stick everything in a bread roll and tuck in.

SPICY STIR-FRIED BEEF

I always seem to make far too much rice, so egg fried rice is a great way of using it up. The secret to storing cooked rice is to chill it as fast possible. As for the first recipe, for spicy stir-fried beef, this is one of my favorites and it never fails to impress and satisfy. Winning combination.

7 oz [200 g] top round or sirloin
   steak

Marinade
2 garlic cloves, crushed
1 tsp fresh cilantro, minced
1 hot chile, thinly sliced
2 Tbsp dark soy sauce
1 Tbsp rice wine
2 tsp superfine sugar
1 Tbsp cornstarch

Rice
¾ cup [150 g] basmati rice
1¼ cups [300 ml] cold water

Sauce
2 Tbsp dark soy sauce
1½ tsp sugar
Squeeze of lime juice
Dash of toasted sesame oil

Stir-fry
1 Tbsp peanut oil
2 tsp toasted sesame oil
3 scallions, cut into ⅜-in [1-cm]
   circles
Fresh cilantro, to serve
Thinly sliced red chile, to serve
   (optional)

Trim any fat off the steak and cut it into ¼-in [½-cm] thick slices across the grain. Put it into a bowl with the marinade ingredients and let it marinate for at least 30 minutes.

Rinse the rice, then put it in a saucepan with the water. Bring it to a boil, cover, and simmer over low heat for 10 minutes, or until the water has been absorbed. Remove from the heat and let stand.

Meanwhile, mix the ingredients for the sauce.

Once your rice is under way and your beef has marinated, heat a wok over very high heat and add the peanut and sesame oils. When very hot, add half the marinated beef. Do not overcrowd the pan; the steak needs to be brown and cook very quickly to keep it tender. Remove it from the wok and keep it warm while you fry the other batch. Remove that and keep it warm, too.

Lower the heat, add the scallions, and cook for 1 to 2 minutes. Add all the beef, the sauce, and any remaining marinade. Heat for another minute.

Drain the rice and fluff it with a fork. Spoon half of it into a bowl and top with the stir-fry and a little more cilantro and chile, if desired.

Let your leftover rice cool and refrigerate it for the next recipe.

2 FOR 1

COOK ³/₄ CUP [150 G] RICE IN THE FIRST RECIPE AND USE THE LEFTOVERS IN THE NEXT RECIPE.

EGG FRIED RICE WITH GARLIC BROCCOLI

½ to 1 small head of broccoli
Scant 1¼ cups [200 g] leftover chilled cooked rice from recipe
    on page 68
Dash of toasted sesame oil
2 Tbsp peanut oil
2 garlic cloves, crushed
2 Tbsp hoisin sauce
2 eggs
1 scallion, thinly sliced
Scant ½ cup [50 g] frozen peas
1 Tbsp dark soy sauce
Fresh cilantro, to serve

Steam the broccoli until almost cooked, 4 to 5 minutes. Heat the sesame oil and a dash of peanut oil in a frying pan over medium heat, then add the garlic and sweat for a few minutes. Once done, add the steamed broccoli and hoisin sauce. Cook for a few minutes until the broccoli is tender. Keep warm while you do the rice.

Beat the eggs in a bowl and add the scallion. Heat the rest of the peanut oil in a wok over medium heat, add the peas, and stir-fry for a minute or so until defrosted. Reduce the heat to low and add the eggs and scallion. Quickly mix with fork or spoon to break it up as it cooks. Before it sets, add the rice and stir well. Add the soy sauce and heat for a minute or two until the rice is piping hot.

Plate up by piling the rice high and topping with the broccoli and a few leaves of cilantro.

POSH BEEF AND TATTIES

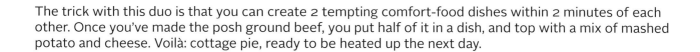

The trick with this duo is that you can create 2 tempting comfort-food dishes within 2 minutes of each other. Once you've made the posh ground beef, you put half of it in a dish, and top with a mix of mashed potato and cheese. Voilà: cottage pie, ready to be heated up the next day.

about 1 Tbsp [4 g] dried porcini mushrooms
7 Tbsp [100 ml] boiling water
14 oz [400 g] ground beef
1 small onion
1 carrot
3 slices of lean bacon
1 Tbsp olive oil
Small piece of butter
2 garlic cloves, crushed
5 Tbsp [75 ml] red wine
2 Tbsp tomato paste
½ tsp yeast extract (Vegemite or Marmite)
Small pinch of dried oregano
Small pinch of dried thyme
Sea salt and freshly ground black pepper

Mashed potato
1¾ lb [800 g] potatoes
2 to 4 Tbsp butter
A splash of milk

Put the dried porcini mushrooms and boiling water in a bowl and let soak for at least 20 minutes. Take the ground beef out of the refrigerator to let it come to room temperature.

For the mashed potato, peel the potatoes and cut into chunks. Put them in a saucepan of cold salted water. Put this onto boil when you start cooking the ground beef.

Mince the onion, carrot, and bacon. Heat the olive oil and butter in a large frying pan over low heat. Add the onion and garlic and sweat for 5 minutes, stirring frequently. Add the carrot and cook for another 5 minutes, or until it softens a little.

Add the bacon and cook slowly until the fat begins to run. Drain the porcini in a strainer over a bowl, keeping the liquid. Chop up the mushrooms and add to the pan, then increase the heat a little. Break up the ground beef with your fingers in a bowl. Add it to the pan and let brown. Keep the heat low to keep it tender. (Remember to start cooking the potatoes now.)

Add the wine and reserved mushroom soaking water and bring to low simmer. Add the tomato paste, yeast extract, and herbs. Stir well. Simmer, uncovered, for about 7 minutes, stirring occasionally.

The potatoes are likely to be done before the meat, so keep them in a warm place or covered with a dish towel. Add the butter and milk, season to taste with salt and pepper, and mash well.

To serve, dollop half the mash artfully in a bowl, top with half the ground beef, and add a quick red-wine or red currant jelly gravy or a horseradish cream, if desired.

2 FOR 1

BUY 14 OZ [400 G] GROUND BEEF, COOK IT IN THE FIRST RECIPE, AND USE THE LEFTOVERS IN THE NEXT RECIPE.

COTTAGE PIE

Leftover cooked ground beef and mashed potato from recipe left
Scant ½ cup [50 g] grated cheddar cheese

Spoon the cooked ground beef into a little ceramic dish. Mix the mashed potato with the grated cheddar and dollop on top of the beef.

Let cool, then refrigerate until ready to heat up the next day. Cook in a preheated oven at 400 °F [200 °C] for 30 minutes.

ROAST BEEF

Four beef beauties from one joint. Cook the roast alongside whatever veg you fancy—parboiled potatoes, carrots, parsnips, etc. The other stars here are a classic spaghetti bolognese, a sumptuous gravy-soaked hot beef sandwich, and a refreshing Vietnamese-style beef pho. Remember to keep the gravy from the roast as it is key for the other dishes in place of broth.

2¼ lb [1 kg] beef top round
    roast
Olive oil, for roasting
2 cups [500 ml] water or broth of
    your choice
Sea salt and freshly ground black
    pepper
Horseradish sauce, to serve

Preheat the oven to 445°F [230°C].

Let the beef come to room temperature if possible. Rub it all over with olive oil and season well with salt and pepper. Heat a frying pan over high heat. Once smoking, add the beef and brown the whole roast.

Once browned, remove the beef to a roasting tray. Roast in the preheated oven for 15 minutes, then reduce the oven temperature to 350°F [180°C] and cook for another 30 to 35 minutes for medium rare, or 45 minutes to 1 hour for medium to well done.

Let the beef rest for at least 5 minutes. Meanwhile, add the water or broth to the roasting tray and set over medium heat on the stove. Scrape any lovely bits off the bottom, bring to a boil, and simmer for 5 minutes. Slice the beef and serve with a good dollop of horseradish sauce and glorious gravy.

4 FOR 1

BUY 2¼ LB [1 KG] TOP ROUND, COOK IT IN THE FIRST RECIPE, AND USE LEFTOVERS IN THE FOLLOWING RECIPES.

SPAG BOL

5¼ to 7 oz [150 to 200 g] leftover
    roasted beef top round roast from
    recipe on page 75
2 slices of lean bacon
Olive oil, for frying
1 small onion, finely diced
1 garlic clove, crushed
1 small carrot, grated
1 celery stalk, very thinly sliced
    (optional)
7 Tbsp [100 ml] red wine
14-oz [400-g] can chopped
    tomatoes
Pinch of fresh or dried thyme
Pinch of sugar
3 to 7 Tbsp [50 to 100 ml] leftover
    gravy, broth, or water
About 2¾ oz [75 g] spaghetti
Sea salt and freshly ground black
    pepper
Grated Parmesan, to serve

Chop the beef into very small pieces, roughly ⅛ to ¼ in [¼ to ½ cm].

Cut the bacon into ⅜-in [1-cm] pieces. Heat a little olive oil in a saucepan over low heat and gently fry the bacon for 2 to 3 minutes.

Add the onion, garlic, and carrot and cook for another 5 to 6 minutes until softened.

Add the wine and cook gently until it has reduced by half. Now add the tomatoes, thyme, sugar, and chopped beef along with the gravy, broth, or water if you think the mixture is too dry. Season lightly with salt and pepper and let bubble away very gently for 20 to 30 minutes until the flavors come together.

At this stage, cook the spaghetti according to the package directions. Check the bolognese seasoning and serve on the spaghetti. Top with grated Parmesan.

BIG COOK
LEFTOVERS

HOT BEEF SANDWICH

7 Tbsp [100 ml] leftover gravy from
   recipe on page 75, or beef broth
3½ oz [100 g] leftover roasted beef
   top round from recipe on page 75,
   thinly sliced
Ciabatta bun or equivalent
Horseradish sauce
Small handful of watercress
   (optional)

Heat the leftover gravy or broth in a frying pan over medium heat until just simmering. Add the sliced beef and let heat through for about 1 minute.

Meanwhile, cut your ciabatta bun through the middle and spread one side generously with horseradish sauce. Top with the watercress.

Remove the beef from the pan with tongs and place on the horseradish side of the bun. Pour over the desired amount of hot gravy or broth on either just the bottom bun or over the whole thing. This is a knife and fork job.

VIETNAMESE-STYLE PHO

¾-in [2-cm] piece of ginger, peeled
2 garlic cloves, peeled
3 cups [750 ml] beef broth
1 star anise
3½ oz [100 g] leftover roasted beef
    top round from recipe on page 75
About 1¾ oz [50 g] rice noodles
½ red onion
1 red chile
Squeeze of lime juice
Small handful of fresh cilantro, torn
Small handful of fresh mint, torn
Fish sauce (optional)

Chop the ginger in half, and bash the garlic with a side of a knife once so it cracks.

Put the broth in a saucepan with the ginger, garlic, and star anise. Bring to a boil and simmer, covered, for 20 minutes. Add the noodles to the broth at the appropriate point, according to the cooking time given in the package directions.

Meanwhile, slice the beef as thinly as possible, and also thinly slice the red onion and chile.

Once the broth has had its time, fish out the noodles and put them in a bowl, then cover with the beef. Pour in the hot broth. Top with the onion, lime juice, cilantro, mint, and chile. Add a little fish sauce to the broth, if desired.

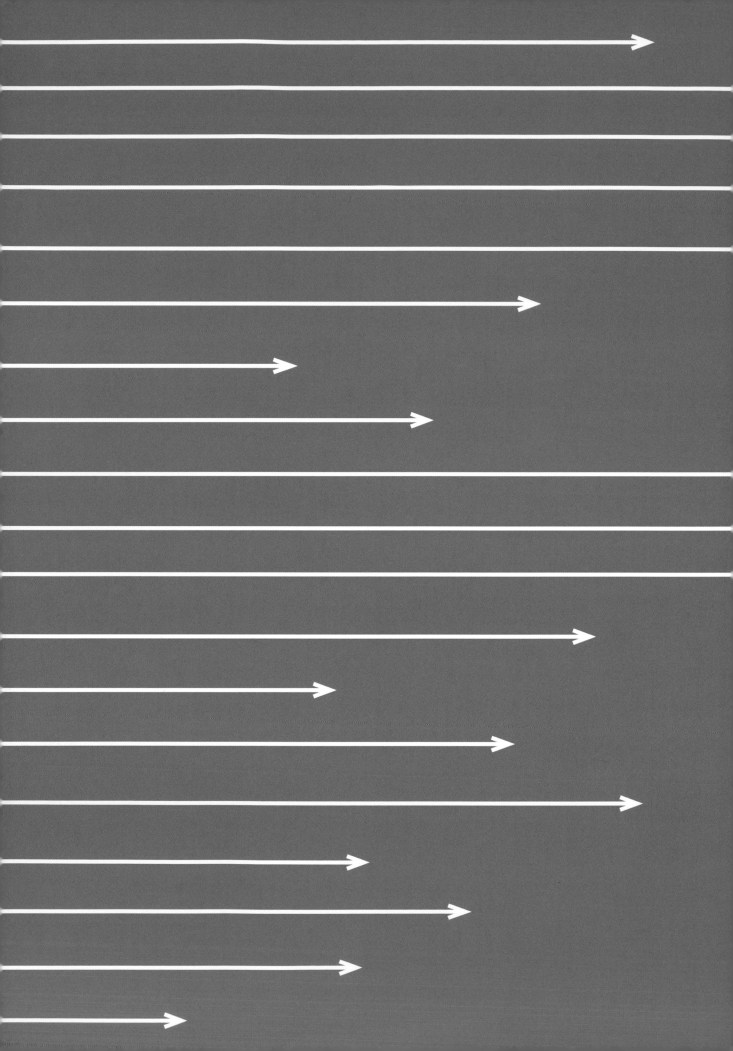

COOK PORK

HARISSA PORK
WITH MANGO AND CILANTRO COUSCOUS

Pork tenderloin is my Dad's favorite because it's a lean hunk of meat, and he's always asking me to cook it, so these pages will have their corners turned down by him for sure! If you have time, marinate the pork for the first recipe for up to 24 hours and it will give it an amazing depth—but it's still fantastic even if you use it straightaway. The key to the leftover stir-fry is the use of dried black fungus, and the chili and garlic sauce. They will give the dish an authentic taste in under 20 minutes.

2 tsp rose harissa paste
Good squeeze of lemon juice
Olive oil, for frying
14 oz [400 g] pork tenderloin, at room temperature
⅝ cup [150 ml] boiling chicken broth
⅓ cup [60 g] couscous
1 mango, sliced into chunks
Handful of fresh cilantro, minced
Sea salt and freshly ground black pepper

Preheat the oven to 350°F [180°C].

Rub the harissa, lemon juice, and olive oil over the pork.

Pour the boiling chicken broth over the couscous in a heatproof bowl; the broth should come ⅛ in [¼ cm] above the couscous. Cover with a clean dish towel and set aside.

Put a little oil in an ovenproof saucepan over high heat and add the pork. Brown it off until light golden on each side, then whack the pan in the oven and cook for 8 to 10 minutes, or until cooked through, depending on the size of the tenderloin.

Meanwhile, once the couscous has absorbed all the water and is nice and fluffy, run a fork through it. Add the mango, cilantro, a little oil, and season with salt and pepper.

Once the pork is cooked, let it rest for 2 to 3 minutes. Halve it and set aside for the next recipe. Slice the remaining half into circles and serve beside the couscous.

2 FOR 1

BUY 14 OZ [400 G] PORK TENDERLOIN, COOK IT IN THE FIRST RECIPE, AND USE THE LEFTOVERS IN THE NEXT RECIPE.

SWEET CHILI PORK STIR-FRY WITH BLACK FUNGUS

¼ oz [5 g] dried black fungus
7 oz [200 g] leftover cooked harissa pork from recipe on page 84
1 tsp chili and garlic sauce (I use Lee Kum Kee)
2 tsp water
1 tsp oyster sauce
Peanut oil, for frying

Put the dried black fungus in a heatproof bowl and cover with boiling water. Let soak for at least 15 minutes. Meanwhile, slice the pork into ⅛-in [¼-cm] wide lengths. Prepare some rice and green vegetables to serve alongside.

Mix the chili and garlic sauce, water, and oyster sauce. Drain the mushrooms and cut off and discard any tough stalks.

In a wok or frying pan over high heat, add a drizzle of oil. Add the pork and stir for a minute or until hot all the way through. Add the mushrooms and cook for another 30 seconds. Lower the heat slightly and add the sauce. Stir and cook for 30 seconds. Serve with the rice and vegetables.

CHINESE SLOW-COOKED PORK

This is an easy and authentic Chinese pair. The slow-cooked pork belly is ideal to cook on a Sunday, as it takes little effort but needs a long time in the oven. The salad is a perfect lunchbox bonus for the Monday after.

1¼ to 1½ lb [600 to 700 g] pork belly
5 scallions
2-in [5-cm] piece of ginger, peeled
4 Tbsp brown sugar
4 Tbsp rice wine
2 Tbsp light soy sauce
2 Tbsp dark soy sauce
⅝ cup [150 ml] water
2 Tbsp peanut oil

Boil some water in a frying pan that will hold your pork belly and be deep enough to cover three-quarters of it. Add the pork and blanch it in the boiling water for 10 minutes.

Meanwhile, chop the scallions into ¾-in [2-cm] long sticks and the ginger into ⅜-in [1-cm] long sticks. Combine with the rest of the ingredients, except the oil, in a Dutch oven or heavy-bottom saucepan.

Remove the blanched pork from the pan and dry it well with paper towels. Heat the peanut oil in a frying pan over very high heat and brown the pork, skin down, until it is very crisp and deeply golden, about 3 to 5 minutes. Remove from the pan and set aside.

Bring the ingredients in the Dutch oven to a boil, stirring to dissolve the sugar. Add the pork, cover, and simmer gently for 1 hour 30 minutes, or until very tender.

Remove the pork from the dish and slice up half of it. Plate it up, pour over the sauce from the dish, and serve it with fluffy white rice and simple green vegetables. Let the remaining pork cool, then cover and refrigerate until ready to use in the next recipe.

2 FOR 1

BUY A PIECE OF PORK BELLY, COOK IT IN THE FIRST RECIPE, AND USE THE LEFTOVERS IN THE NEXT RECIPE.

PORK BELLY SALAD
WITH SPICY SESAME DRESSING

Leftover cooked pork belly from recipe above
1 garlic clove, minced
1 scallion, minced
½ tsp sugar
2 Tbsp light soy sauce
Drizzle of toasted sesame oil
½ to 1 tsp chili oil
Handful of lettuce leaves
4-in [10-cm] piece of cucumber

Slice the pork belly into thin strips, removing the fat if desired. Mix the garlic, scallion, sugar, soy sauce, sesame oil, and chili oil together in a small bowl. Shred the lettuce and cut the cucumber into thin sticks.

Plate up the lettuce and cucumber, top with the pork, and pour over the dressing.

CHOPS, CHORIZO, AND CHEESE

Pork and apple are the classic combo here. And then when you smother the chops with cheese and chorizo, it becomes naughty; served with French fries, this is proper hangover food! Then the leftover pork is turned into a hog-roast-style sandwich by making the quickest applesauce ever.

2 pork chops
Olive oil, for frying and dressing
1 oz [25 g] chorizo
1 apple, peeled and cored
Handful of raisins
Squeeze of lemon juice
1 slice of cheddar cheese
Sea salt and freshly ground black
   pepper

Preheat the oven to 400°F [200°C].

Coat the pork chops with olive oil and season well with salt and pepper. Heat an ovenproof frying pan over medium-high heat, then add the pork chops and brown well, about 1 minute each side. Make sure you sear the fat as well. Slick the pan in the preheated oven for 10 to 15 minutes, depending on thickness, or until cooked through.

Peel the chorizo and chop it into small dice. Slice the apple into small thin sticks, then mix it with the raisins, lemon juice, and a drizzle of olive oil.

One minute before the pork is ready, pile one of the chops high with the chorizo and top with the cheese. Put it back in the oven for the remaining minute, then let rest for a couple more.

Pile the apple salad onto a plate with the pork chop on one side. Let the other pork chop cool, then cover and refrigerate until ready to use in the next recipe.

2 FOR 1

BUY 2 PORK CHOPS, COOK THEM IN THE FIRST RECIPE, AND USE THE LEFTOVERS IN THE NEXT RECIPE.

PORK SANDWICH WITH QUICK APPLESAUCE

1 apple, peeled and cored
½ to 1 tsp sugar
1 leftover cooked pork chop from
   recipe above
1 bread bun or 2 slices of bread
Butter, softened

Cut the apple into ⅜-in [1-cm] chunks. Place in a microwaveable bowl with the sugar, cover, and microwave for 3 to 4 minutes until soft. (Or, cook it in a pan for 10 to 20 minutes.) Blitz with a hand blender or food processor, or mash with a fork. Let cool, if desired.

Remove the fat from the pork and thinly slice the meat. Butter the bread, lay the pork on top, and smother in applesauce.

CHORIZO AND SWEET POTATO SOUP

First we have a very simple and inexpensive soup that makes enough for 2 servings—excellent!
Chorizo also plays a starring role in the full-power omelet up next.

14 oz [400 g] sweet potato
1¾ oz [50 g] chorizo
Olive oil, for frying
1 small onion, diced
1 garlic clove, crushed
2½ cups [600 ml] hot chicken broth
Sea salt and freshly ground black
   pepper

Peel the sweet potato and chop it into ¾-in [2-cm] chunks. Peel the
chorizo and slice it into ⅜-in [1-cm] thick circles, then slice those in half
to make semicircles.

Heat a little olive oil in a frying pan over medium heat and fry the
chorizo until golden brown. Remove the chorizo from the pan. Throw
in the onion and garlic and sweat over low heat, stirring regularly, for 4 to
5 minutes. Add the sweet potato, chorizo, and broth and simmer gently,
covered, for 10 to 15 minutes until the sweet potato is cooked.

Blend the contents of the pan with a hand blender (or let it cool a bit
then process it in a blender or food processor) until smooth. Season to
taste with salt and pepper.

2 FOR 1

BUY 2³/₄ OZ [75 G] CHORIZO AND COOK SOME IN THE FIRST RECIPE AND THE REST IN THE NEXT RECIPE.

CHORIZO, FETA, AND RED PEPPER OMELET

1 oz [25 g] chorizo
1¼ oz [35 g] feta
1 roasted red bell pepper from a jar, drained
3 eggs
Splash of water
Freshly ground black pepper
Olive oil, for frying

Peel the chorizo and chop it into small dice. Chop the feta into small dice, too, and slice the pepper into thin strips. Crack the eggs into a bowl, add a splash of water, and beat lightly with a fork.

Heat a little olive oil in a frying pan over medium heat and fry the chorizo until golden brown.

Add the feta and pepper to the eggs. Season with pepper. Tip the egg mixture into the pan over the chorizo and let cook, pulling the sides back with a spatula and then tipping runny egg into the space.

When the omelet is cooked through (you can flash it under a hot broiler for a minute to brown the top if desired), tip it onto a plate, folding it in half at the same time if you have the knack!

SAUSAGE, MASH, AND GRAVY

A firm old friend—absolutely everyone is cheerful about sausage and mash on the menu! The breakfast hash that follows is a hot contender for my favorite-ever breakfast. It is also great for using up any leftovers you have lying around, as it works well with cooked veg, such as broccoli.

6 sausages
1¼ lb [550 g] potatoes, peeled
Olive oil, for frying
Squeeze of lemon juice
1 to 2 Tbsp butter
Splash of milk
Mustard (optional)
Sea salt and freshly ground black
    pepper

Red wine gravy
1 small onion
3 heaping Tbsp [50 ml] red wine
⅞ cup [200 ml] hot chicken broth
1 tsp cornstarch
1 tsp water

2 FOR 1

BUY 6 SAUSAGES AND 1¹/₄ LB [550 G] POTATOES, COOK THEM IN THE FIRST RECIPE, AND USE THE LEFTOVERS IN THE NEXT RECIPE.

Preheat the oven to 400°F [200°C].

Cook the sausages on a rack over a roasting tray in the preheated oven for 25 minutes, or until cooked through.

Meanwhile, cut the potatoes into quarters and place in a saucepan of cold water. Bring to a boil and cook for another 15 minutes, or until they are mashable.

For the gravy, thinly slice the onion. Heat a good drizzle of olive oil in a frying pan over low heat, then fry the onion, stirring regularly for 10 to 15 minutes until it turns golden brown. Add the red wine and cook for a minute, then add the broth. Mix the cornstarch and water until smooth. Add this to the pan and cook on a gentle simmer for 5 to 10 minutes, or until you're ready to plate up. Season with salt and pepper to taste.

Drain the cooked potatoes and transfer about 5¼ oz [150 g] of them (roughly half a large potato) to a plate with a squeeze of lemon juice. To the remaining potatoes add the butter, milk, and some seasoning and mash to your liking. Add a bit of mustard, if desired.

Plate up 3 to 4 sausages on top of the mash and cover in gravy. Put the remaining sausages and the reserved potato to one side to cool, then cover and refrigerate until ready to use in the next recipe.

BREAKFAST HASH

2 to 3 leftover cooked sausages
    from recipe above
3 mushrooms
1 garlic clove, crushed
5¼ oz [150 g] leftover cooked
    potato from recipe above,
    grated
1 egg
Olive oil, for frying
Butter, for frying
Sea salt and freshly ground
    black pepper

Preheat the broiler for the egg if you want it extra fast.

Slice the cooked sausages and the mushrooms into ⅜-in [1-cm] thick circles. Heat a little olive oil and butter in a frying pan over low heat and sweat the garlic for a minute or so. Add the mushrooms and cook for 2 to 3 minutes. Add the sausages and warm through for 2 minutes. Add the potato and cook for 2 minutes until piping hot.

Crack an egg over the top and cook for 5 minutes, or until set. Alternatively, whack it under the broiler if you are impatient (and if your frying pan is ovenproof!). Season with salt and pepper and enjoy.

SAUSAGE AND LENTIL STEW

A delightful French winter dish, this stew costs little and is mightily satisfying ... And the same can be said for the Italian-inspired sausage pasta. A tasty Mediterranean duo. The best sausages for these, if you can find them, are Toulouse sausages, or those with apple in them.

Olive oil, for frying
3 sausages
1 onion, diced
1 large garlic clove, crushed
7 Tbsp [100 ml] red wine
3 heaping Tbsp [50 ml] water
14-oz [400-g] can cooked green lentils, drained and rinsed
Sea salt and freshly ground black pepper
Crusty bread, to serve

Heat a little olive oil in a saucepan over medium heat, then add the sausages and fry until evenly browned. Remove them from the pan.

Add the onion and garlic to the pan and sweat over very low heat for 4 to 5 minutes. Add the wine, water, lentils, and sausages. Cover and bring to a boil, then simmer gently for about 20 minutes, or until the sausages are cooked through. Season to taste.

Spoon into a bowl and serve with crusty bread.

2 FOR 1

BUY 6 TOULOUSE OR PORK
AND APPLE SAUSAGES AND
COOK HALF IN EACH RECIPE.

SAUSAGE AND MUSTARD PASTA

2 to 3 sausages
1 heaping tsp whole grain mustard
1 Tbsp honey
1 Tbsp orange juice
3½ oz [100 g] pasta of your choice
1 Tbsp crème fraîche
Squeeze of lemon juice
Sea salt and freshly ground black pepper

Preheat the oven to 400°F [200°C] and put a large saucepan of cold water, with a dash of salt, onto boil for the pasta.

Place the sausages in a small roasting tray. Mix together the mustard, honey, and orange juice, then pour over the sausages. Bake in the preheated oven for 20 to 25 minutes, turning and coating 3 times until the sausages are cooked.

Put the pasta in the pan of boiling water at this stage and cook it according to the package directions to coincide with the sausages being cooked.

Once the sausages are cooked, slice them into ⅜- to ¾-in [1- to 2-cm] chunks, then return them to the tray and roll to coat them in the honey mixture. Drain the pasta and return to the pan along with the crème fraîche. Stir well to coat, then plate up with the sausages. Add the lemon juice and a grind of pepper.

MAPLE-GLAZED HAM STEAK

Ham steak is thrifty and very tasty. Maple syrup is more than just for pancakes—and here it provides a sweet glaze which beautifully counterbalances the saltiness of the ham. With the leftovers you can make delicious spaghetti carbonara, which has to be one of the most straightforward yet flavorsome dinners ever.

7 oz [200 g] rutabaga, peeled
7 oz [200 g] potato, peeled
10½ oz [300 g] ham steak
Olive oil, for frying
Small piece of butter
Splash of milk
Sea salt and freshly ground
    black pepper

Maple glaze
1 tsp cider vinegar
1 tsp English mustard
2 tsp maple syrup

Cut the rutabaga and potato into ⅜-in [1-cm] chunks. Put the rutabaga into a saucepan of cold water and bring to a boil. Once boiling, cook for another 5 minutes, then add the potato. Cook for 15 minutes, or until both the rutabaga and potato are cooked.

Meanwhile, mix the ingredients for the maple glaze.

Lightly coat the ham steak in olive oil. Heat a frying pan over medium-high heat and cook the ham for 1 minutes each side. Lower the heat and baste the steak with a little of the glaze. Cook for 2 to 3 minutes each side, basting and turning twice. Watch that the glaze doesn't catch, and turn the heat down if it does. Once cooked, baste once more and then let rest.

Mash the rutabaga and potato with the butter, milk, and some salt and pepper. Cut off about one-quarter of the ham and set aside to cool before refrigerating until ready to use in the second recipe.

Plate up the remaining ham and the mash and enjoy!

2 FOR 1

BUY 10½ OZ [300 G] HAM STEAK, COOK IT IN THE FIRST RECIPE, AND USE THE LEFTOVERS IN THE NEXT RECIPE.

SPAGHETTI CARBONARA

3½ oz [100 g] spaghetti
1¾ oz [50 g] leftover cooked ham
    steak from recipe above
1 large egg yolk
Scant ¼ cup [25 g] grated
    Parmesan cheese, plus extra
    to serve
Sea salt and freshly ground
    black pepper

Put a large saucepan of salted water onto boil. Once boiling, add the spaghetti and cook according to the package directions.

Cut the ham into small pieces, removing any fat. Once the spaghetti is almost cooked, mix the egg yolk with the Parmesan and a good amount of black pepper. Add a little warm water at the last minute to loosen the mixture.

Drain the cooked spaghetti, setting the water it was cooked in aside. Toss the spaghetti with the egg mixture and meat. Add a spoonful or two of the hot water to create more of a sauce. Serve with a little more grated Parmesan on top.

SAUSAGE MEATBALLS AND PASTA
IN A SPICY TOMATO SAUCE

These two are cheap cheats—they cost next to nothing and are very easy to make. The sausages are transformed into minute meatballs, and the can of beans takes all the time and effort out of the cassoulet—well, that's just downright cheeky. But it works, so why not!?

Olive oil, for frying
2 garlic cloves, crushed
*14-oz [400-g] can chopped
    tomatoes*
Pinch of sugar
½ to 1 tsp dried red pepper flakes
½ tsp dried oregano (optional)
3 sausages
3½ oz [100 g] pasta of your choice
*Sea salt and freshly ground black
    pepper*
Grated Parmesan, to serve

Heat a little olive oil in a saucepan over low heat, then gently sweat the garlic for a couple of minutes. Add the tomatoes, sugar, red pepper flakes, and oregano and simmer very gently for 10 to 15 minutes.

Run a small, sharp knife down the length of the sausages and pull off the skin. Divide each sausage into 3 pieces and roll each one into balls. Put a large saucepan of cold water, with a dash of salt, onto boil for the pasta.

Heat a little more oil in a frying pan over medium heat, brown the meatballs in a little oil. Once the sauce has had its time to simmer, add the meatballs and cook, covered, for 15 minutes, or until they are cooked through. Season with salt and pepper. Put the pasta in the pan of boiling water at this stage and cook it according to the package directions to coincide with the meatballs being cooked.

Plate up the pasta, spoon over the sauce and meatballs, and be generous with the grated Parmesan.

2 FOR 1

BUY 6 SAUSAGES AND COOK HALF IN EACH RECIPE.

QUICK CASSOULET

Olive oil, for frying
3 sausages (I use Toulouse sausages)
1¾ oz [50 g] chorizo
1 small onion, diced
2 garlic cloves, crushed
7 Tbsp [100 ml] cider or apple juice
Scant 1¼ cups [200 g] baked beans
¼ tsp mustard
3 to 7 Tbsp [50 to 100 ml] water
1 slice of white bread
Handful of fresh parsley
Sea salt and freshly ground black pepper

Heat a little olive oil in a heavy-bottom saucepan or Dutch oven over medium heat, then add the sausages and fry until brown all over. Remove the sausages from the pan.

Peel the chorizo and slice it into ⅜-in [1-cm] thick circles, then slice those in half to make semicircles. Add the chorizo to the pan and brown, too, then remove.

Add a little more oil to the pan, if needed, and sweat the onion and garlic over low heat for 4 to 5 minutes, stirring regularly. Add the cider, beans, and mustard and stir. Add the sausages and cook for 20 minutes at a gentle simmer. Stir regularly and add the water if it's looking too dry and sticking. Add the chorizo and cook for another 5 minutes. Season to taste with salt and pepper.

Meanwhile, blitz up the bread and parsley in a food processor to make bread crumbs. Preheat the broiler.

Once the cassoulet is cooked, transfer it to an ovenproof dish if what it's in is not already ovenproof. Scatter the bread crumbs over the cassoulet and drizzle with a little olive oil. Broil until golden, then serve.

ROAST PORK BELLY

Here you start off with a delightful piece of pork belly roasted with apples, which become succulent and gorgeous. This is followed by a reunion of the pork and apple in the form of potato cakes—perfect lunchtime snacks. Then for something completely different but just as divine: a satay pork sandwich, the lunchbox king. Finally we've a pork and split pea soup after the Dutch *snert*. My version is a big brassy filler, a winter warmer that's thick and flavorsome from which you'll get several servings.

2¼ lb [1 kg] pork belly
2 apples, cut in half
Sea salt
10½ to 15¾ oz [300 to 450 g]
 potatoes, quartered and parboiled
⅝ cup [150 ml] cider, apple juice, or
 broth of your choice
3 to 4 fresh sage leaves (optional)

Preheat the oven to 425°F [220°C]. Wipe the pork belly dry with paper towels.

Score the pork skin deeply with a small, sharp knife—but not so deeply that you get through to hit flesh—at ⅜-in [1-cm] intervals. Place the pork in a roasting tray with room to spare, and rub a generous amount of salt into the skin. Roast in the preheated oven for 30 minutes. Reduce the oven temperature to 350°F [180°C] and roast for 40 to 50 minutes. Now add the parboiled potatoes around the pork and 20 minutes later, add the apples, cut side down. After the time is up, the meat should be very soft and the skin crisp.

Remove the meat from the tray and let rest for 10 minutes before carving. Remove the potatoes and apples, too. Pour the cider, apple juice, or broth into the tray, set over medium heat on the stove and bring to a boil, scraping up any lovely bits to incorporate them into the gravy. Boil until reduced by about half and season to taste with salt and pepper. Carve about a quarter of the pork for yourself now, plate up 2 halves of apple, and your roasties. Be liberal with the gravy. Let the remaining pork and apples cool, then cover and refrigerate until ready to use in the following recipes.

4 FOR 1

BUY 2¹/₄ LB (1 KG) PORK BELLY, COOK IT IN THE FIRST RECIPE, AND USE THE LEFTOVERS IN THE FOLLOWING RECIPES.

PORK, APPLE, AND SAGE POTATO CAKES

2 halves of leftover baked apple from recipe on page 100

¾ to scant 1 cup [175 to 200 g] mashed potato (use leftovers from another meal, or make it from leftover boiled or roast potatoes following page 72)

1¾ oz [50 g] leftover roasted pork belly from recipe on page 100, shredded

1 tsp fresh sage, minced

1 egg, beaten (optional)

1 to 2 Tbsp all-purpose flour

Olive oil, for frying

Sea salt and freshly ground black pepper

Remove the skin from the baked apple halves and cut into small dice. Combine with the mashed potato, pork, and sage, and season with salt and pepper. Form into 2 patties. If the mixture is too dry and won't come together, add some beaten egg.

Put the flour on a plate and dip each side of the potato cake in to coat it lightly with flour. Heat a little olive oil in a frying pan over medium heat, then fry the potato cakes for 3 to 4 minutes each side, or until piping hot and golden brown.

SATAY PORK SANDWICH

1 bread roll
2¾ oz [75 g] leftover roasted belly
   pork from recipe on page 100,
   shredded
A few very thin slices of cucumber
Small handful of fresh cilantro
A few very thin slices of red onion

Satay sauce
1 Tbsp cider vinegar
1 tsp sugar
14-oz [400-g] can coconut milk
2 tsp Thai red curry paste
1½ Tbsp smooth peanut butter
½ Tbsp dark soy sauce

Mix the ingredients for the satay sauce together in a saucepan over low heat. Whisk until combined and simmer gently for 4 minutes. Let cool if desired.

Cut the bread roll in half and add the shredded pork, the cucumber, cilantro, and red onion. Spoon on as much satay sauce as you wish. Eat!

The satay sauce will keep for over a week in the refrigerator if covered properly; use as a sauce on any meat for a delicious treat.

BIG COOK LEFTOVERS

PORK AND SPLIT PEA SOUP

1 small carrot
1 small onion
1 celery stalk
Olive oil, for frying
2½ cups [250 g] split peas, washed
3 cups [750 ml] hot chicken broth
2¾ oz [75 g] leftover roasted belly
    pork from recipe on page 100
Frankfurters—1 per portion
Sea salt and freshly ground black
    pepper

Cut the carrot, onion, and celery into small dice. Heat a glug of olive oil in a saucepan over low heat, then fry the carrot, onion, and celery for about 10 minutes, or until they start to soften.

Add the split peas to the pan, mix, then add the hot chicken broth. Cover the pan and simmer gently for 1 hour.

Meanwhile, shred the pork. When the soup has been simmering for 1 hour, add the shredded pork and the frankfurter(s) to the pan and let cook for 4 minutes.

Ladle into a bowl and serve with a slice of toast spread with mustard. Let the leftover soup cool, then cover and refrigerate to enjoy another day.

COOK

Lamb

Rack of Lamb
with couscous and griddled eggplant

Rack of lamb is tender, lean, and tasty, and cooking it on the bone adds extra flavor. Customize your couscous by improvising with what you have, such as fresh or sundried tomatoes, olives, harissa, herbs feta, and so much more. In the salad recipe, the cheese gives an appealing flavor counterbalance.

1 small eggplant
Olive oil, for frying
1 lemon
1 extra trimmed rack of lamb, about 10½ oz [300 g]
⅝ cup [150 ml] boiling water
⅓ cup [60 g] couscous
Sea salt and freshly ground black pepper
Optional fillings (see introduction above)

Preheat the oven to 425°F [220°C].

Cut the eggplant into ⅜-in [1-cm] thick slices. Season with salt and pepper and brush both sides lightly with olive oil. Heat a griddle pan until it starts to smoke. Cook the eggplant for 1 to 2 minutes each side, or until golden brown. Remove to a plate and squeeze over some lemon juice.

Pour the boiling water over the couscous in a heatproof bowl; it should come ⅛ in [¼ cm] above the couscous. Cover and set aside.

Drizzle a little oil and lemon juice over the lamb and season it with salt and pepper. Put an ovenproof frying pan over high heat, then sear the lamb for 1 to 2 minutes each side, or until golden brown. Transfer the pan to the oven and cook for 9 to 10 minutes for medium. Remove from the oven and let rest for a few minutes. Meanwhile, once the couscous has absorbed all the water and is nice and fluffy, run a fork through it.

Plate up the couscous (adding any optional fillings) and eggplant. Cut half the lamb into slices and add to the plate. Let the remaining lamb cool, then refrigerate until ready to use in the second recipe.

Warm Lamb Salad

Big handful of frozen fava beans
Leftover cooked rack of lamb from recipe above, at room temperature
Olive oil, for frying
2 Boston lettuces, halved lengthwise
Scant ¼ cup [25 g] grated cheddar
Sea salt and freshly ground black pepper

Dressing
1 Tbsp plain yogurt
1 tsp white wine vinegar
1 tsp olive oil
1 tsp minced fresh mint

Boil the fava beans in a saucepan of water for 6 minutes. Drain and run under cold water, then peel each one to remove the pale green skins. Lightly season them with salt and pepper and set them aside.

If desired, heat the lamb by wrapping it in foil, roasting it at 425°F [220°C] for 10 to 12 minutes, then let rest for a few minutes.

Mix the ingredients for the dressing.

Heat a griddle pan until almost smoking (make sure your extractor fan is on). Rub olive oil over the halved Boston lettuces and season with salt and pepper. Griddle, cut side down, for 2 to 3 minutes until golden brown and charred.

Slice the lamb. Sprinkle the fava beans and grated cheese over a plate. Top with the griddled lettuces, lamb, and dressing.

2 FOR 1

BUY 10½ OZ (300 G) RACK
OF LAMB, COOK IT IN THE
FIRST RECIPE, AND USE
THE LEFTOVERS IN THE
NEXT RECIPE.

Shepherd's Pie

This way with shepherd's pie is a completely new invention! Who would have thought a lamb bread-and-butter pudding could taste so good? Magic seems to happen when the lamb juices get soaked up by the bread and the top becomes crisp. Traditionalists can easily top this with mashed potato instead. If you had any bits and pieces of veg in the refrigerator, you could combine them with the onion and carrot and use them up. Turn the rest of the package of ground lamb into kofta for a touch of the Middle East—especially good for livening up your lunchbox! These recipes are a great ground lamb duo.

Olive oil, for frying
1 small onion, diced
1 small carrot, diced
8¾ oz [250 g] ground lamb
1 to 1¼ cups [250 to 300 ml] beef or chicken broth
1 tsp Worcestershire sauce
1 tsp tomato paste or ketchup
Butter, for spreading
2 slices of white bread
Sea salt and freshly ground black pepper

Heat a glug of olive oil in a heavy-bottom saucepan or Dutch oven over low heat, then sweat the onion and carrot for 5 to 10 minutes until they begin to soften.

Increase the heat and crumble in the ground lamb. Brown for a few minutes. Add 1 cup [250 ml] of the broth, the Worcestershire sauce, and tomato paste or ketchup. Simmer gently for 20 minutes. Add more broth if it seems dry, and stir regularly.

Meanwhile, preheat the oven to 400 °F [200 °C]. Butter the slices of bread generously on one side, then cut into little triangles.

Once the ground lamb is cooked, season with salt and pepper to taste. Spoon it into a small ovenproof dish and top with overlapping triangles of bread, butter side up. Bake in the preheated oven for 10 to 15 minutes until the bread is golden.

2 FOR 1

BUY 1 LB [500 G] GROUND LAMB AND COOK HALF IN EACH RECIPE.

Kofta Wrap

8¾ oz [250 g] ground lamb
1 tsp minced fresh mint
1¼-in [3-cm] piece of ginger, peeled and grated
1 garlic clove, crushed
¾ tsp ground cumin
¾ tsp ground coriander
1 tsp mango chutney
1 Tbsp plain yogurt
1 wrap or pita bread
1 to 2 lettuce leaves
1 tomato, sliced
Sea salt and freshly ground black pepper
1 to 2 metal skewers

Preheat the broiler.

Mix together the ground lamb, mint, ginger, cumin, and coriander. Mold the mixture into 1 or 2 sausage shapes and thread or shape them around the metal skewers. Broil them for 4 minutes each side, or until golden brown and cooked through. Let rest.

Combine the mango chutney and yogurt. Spread on a wrap or inside pita bread and add the lettuce and tomato. Slice the kofta and add it to the wrap or pita. Roll or close to serve. This works beautifully with tzatziki.

Lamb and Mint Burger

Cooking lamb burgers this way lets the fat drip away, which is always a bonus. Feel free to experiment with the burger filling by adding cumin, fennel seed, or rosemary. With the other half of the ground lamb you can make a brilliant, cheap, and authentic curry.

7 oz [200 g] ground lamb
1½ tsp minced fresh mint
1¾ oz [50 g] beet, peeled and grated
1 Tbsp plain yogurt
Squeeze of lemon juice
Arugula, to serve
Tzatziki, to serve
Bread roll
Sea salt and freshly ground black
    pepper

Preheat the broiler.

Mix together the lamb and mint and season well with salt and pepper. Shape into a patty. Place on a rack over a roasting tray and broil for 5 to 7 minutes each side until golden brown and cooked through. Let rest.

Combine the beet, yogurt, and lemon and season to taste with salt and pepper.

Construct your burger: arugula, lamb burger, and tzatziki piled into the bread roll.

2 FOR 1

BUY 1 LB [500 G]
GROUND LAMB AND COOK
HALF IN EACH RECIPE.

Lamb Keema Curry

Peanut oil, for frying
1 red onion, thinly sliced
2 garlic cloves, crushed
1¼-in [3-cm] piece of ginger,
    peeled and grated
1½ to 2 Tbsp balti paste
10½ oz [300 g] ground lamb
⅝ cup [150 ml] water
Handful of frozen peas
1 Tbsp Greek yogurt
Squeeze of lemon juice
Sea salt and freshly ground
    black pepper
Fresh cilantro, to serve

Heat a little peanut oil in a saucepan over low heat, then gently fry the red onion for 10 to 15 minutes. Add the garlic, ginger, and balti paste and cook for another 2 minutes. Add 3 heaping Tbsp [50 ml] of the water and cook until it has evaporated.

Increase the heat and crumble in the ground lamb. Brown for a few minutes. Add the remaining 7 Tbsp [100 ml] water, cover, and simmer gently for 20 minutes.

Add the peas to the pan and cook for 2 minutes. Remove the pan from the heat and stir in the yogurt and lemon juice. Season to taste with salt and pepper. Serve topped with fresh cilantro and accompanied by rice or naan bread.

Garlic and Lemon Chops

First up here is a summery fresh-flavored treat from the Med. Cooking the chops under the broiler gives a hint of BBQ without the fuss. For the other dish, you've pretty much got an instant Chinese delight; superquick, and really tasty.

4 lamb chops
2 garlic cloves, crushed
Juice of ½ lemon
Olive oil, for marinating and
    dressing
⅓ cup [60 g] couscous
⅓ to ½ cup [80 to 120 ml] hot
    chicken broth
2 tsp chopped fresh basil
1 Tbsp black olives, pitted and
    chopped
Sea salt and freshly ground black
    pepper

Preheat the broiler to its highest setting if you are not marinating the lamb overnight.

Put the lamb chops in a shallow bowl with the garlic, lemon juice, and a drizzle of olive oil. Make sure the chops are well coated in the ingredients, then prepare to cook them straightaway, or cover and let marinate for up to 24 hours in the refrigerator. Season the chops with salt and pepper just before cooking.

Put the couscous in a heatproof bowl and pour the hot chicken broth over making sure that it's just less than an inch above the level of the couscous. Cover with a clean dish towel and set to one side.

Broil the lamb chops for 4 to 5 minutes each side until golden brown and cooked to your liking. Let rest.

Once the couscous has been steaming for at least 6 minutes, run a fork through it until it's nice and fluffy. Add a drizzle of oil, the basil, and black olives and season to taste with salt and pepper.

Pile your couscous high and position 2 of the chops on top. Squeeze over a little more lemon, if desired. Serve with tomatoes, salad, or a mix of roasted veg. Let the remaining 2 chops cook, then cover and refrigerate until ready to use in the next recipe.

2 FOR 1

BUY 4 LAMB CHOPS, COOK THEM IN THE FIRST RECIPE, AND USE THE LEFTOVERS IN THE NEXT RECIPE.

Lamb Stir-Fry

2 leftover cooked lamb chops
    from recipe above
4 scallions
¾-in [2-cm] piece of ginger
Peanut oil, for frying
2 garlic cloves, crushed
2 Tbsp hoisin sauce

Remove the meat from the leftover lamb chops and cut into thin slices. Cut the scallions into ¾-in [2-cm] thin sticks. Peel and slice the ginger into thin sticks, too.

Add a good glug of peanut oil to a wok or large frying pan. Once hot, stir-fry the ginger for a couple of minutes. Then add the scallions and garlic and continue to cook for another 2 minutes. Add the lamb, fry for a minute, then add the hoisin sauce and cook for another 30 seconds. Serve on rice.

One-Pot Lamb Stew

Neck needs some clever slow-cooking, but it's dirt cheap and the results are worth it. The spring broth you make with the leftovers, on the other hand, is very quick—a sheer delight ready in just 5 minutes ...

1 lb [500 g] lamb neck
2 Tbsp all-purpose flour, seasoned
    with salt and pepper
Olive oil, for frying
1 small onion, diced
1 garlic clove, crushed
1 small carrot, diced
7 Tbsp [100 ml] white wine
7 oz [200 g] new potatoes, scrubbed
    and halved
3 to 4 fresh rosemary sprigs
1 cup [250 ml] chicken broth
Lemon juice (optional)
Sea salt and freshly ground black
    pepper

Preheat the oven to 325°F [170°C].

Chop the lamb into 1-in [2.5-cm] chunks and dust them in the seasoned flour. Heat a glug of olive oil in a Dutch oven over medium-high heat and add the chunks of lamb in batches (so as not to overcrowd the dish). Brown them well all over, then remove those chunks, add a little more oil if necessary and sear the remaining batches in the same way. Set all the lamb aside.

In the same dish, heat a glug more oil, then sweat the onion, garlic, and carrot for 5 minutes. Add the wine and deglaze the pan for 2 minutes —i.e. scrape any bits off the bottom with a wooden spoon to release all those flavorful little morsels of meat and veg.

Add the potatoes, rosemary, broth, and seared chunks of lamb. Bring to a boil then cook at a gentle simmer, covered, for 1 hour 30 minutes, or until the lamb is incredibly soft. Season with salt and pepper to taste and add a squeeze of lemon juice, if desired. Plate up, setting aside 5 to 6 chunks of lamb (and a few bits of the veg if you fancy). Let cool, then cover and refrigerate until ready to use in the next recipe.

Spring Broth with Lamb

2 cups [500 ml] chicken broth
2 handfuls of chopped kale
3½ oz [100 g] leftover cooked lamb
   from recipe left
Leftover cooked carrots from recipe
   left (optional)
Leftover cooked potatoes from recipe
   left (optional)
Handful of frozen peas

Put the chicken broth in a saucepan and bring to a simmer. Add the kale and cook for about 5 minutes, or until tender.

Meanwhile cut the lamb into smaller chunks and add it to the pan along with any leftover cooked veg. Simmer for another minute. Finally, add the frozen peas and cook for 30 seconds. Ladle into a bowl and serve.

2 FOR 1

BUY 1 LB [500 G] NECK FILLET, COOK IT IN THE FIRST RECIPE, AND USE THE LEFTOVERS IN THE NEXT RECIPE.

Tikka Lamb Chops

Because the lamb and potato are cooked together in this first recipe, the delicious marinated lamb juices are soaked up by the potato and give them a real intensity of flavor. The spiced shallots in the partner recipe are a pickle-tray classic and have a lovely sharp sweetness.

1 Tbsp plain yogurt
3 tsp tikka masala paste
Good squeeze of lemon juice
4 lamb chops
7 oz [200 g] potato, peeled
Peanut oil, for frying
Pinch of mustard seeds
¼ tsp ground turmeric
¼ tsp chili powder
3 heaping Tbsp [50 ml] water
Sea salt and freshly ground black pepper

Combine the yogurt, tikka masala paste, and lemon juice in a shallow bowl. Add the lamb chops and make sure they're well coated in the ingredients. Cover and let marinate for at least 30 minutes, or for up to 24 hours in the refrigerator.

Preheat the oven to 350°F [180°C]. Chop the potato into ⅜-in [1-cm] dice. Heat a good glug of peanut oil in an ovenproof frying pan over high heat. Add the lamb chops and fry for a couple of minutes each side until golden brown. Remove and set aside. Wipe any charred bits from the pan.

Heat 2 Tbsp of the oil in the same pan. Add the mustard seeds, turmeric, and chili when it's hot enough (you can tell if it is by adding one seed; if it pops it's ready). Fry for a minute, stirring as you do. Add the potatoes, stir to coat them in the spices, and season with salt and pepper. Fry them for 5 to 10 minutes until crisp and brown on all sides.

Add the water to the pan and turn off the heat. Place the chops on top and put the pan into the preheated oven. Roast for 14 to 18 minutes, or until the potatoes and lamb are cooked. Finish with a squeeze more lemon juice, to taste. Serve up 2 of the chops on the potatoes. Let the remaining lamb chops cool, then cover and refrigerate until ready to use in the next recipe.

Lamb Potato Cakes

2 leftover cooked lamb chops
Peanut oil, for frying
1 tsp tikka masala paste
1 tsp garam masala
Large handful of frozen peas
1¼ cups [300 g] mashed potato (use leftovers from another meal, or make it from scratch following page 72)
Beaten egg, to bind (optional)
2 Tbsp all-purpose flour, seasoned with salt and pepper
Sea salt and freshly ground black pepper

Spiced shallots
1 shallot, diced
3 Tbsp tomato ketchup
2 tsp mint sauce
1 Tbsp mango chutney
Pinch of salt

Combine the ingredients for the spiced shallots and set aside.

Remove the meat from the leftover lamb chops and chop finely.

Heat a little peanut oil in a saucepan over medium heat and add the tikka masala paste and garam masala. Stir-fry for a minute or so, then add the peas and cook for another minute.

Now add the mashed potato to the pan, remove from the heat, and stir to ensure everything is evenly incorporated. Add the chopped lamb and season with salt and pepper. Form the mixture into 2 to 3 patties, adding the beaten egg if the mixture is too dry to bind.

Coat the patties all over in the seasoned flour. Heat a splash of peanut oil in a frying pan over medium heat, then fry the patties for 4 to 5 minutes each side, or until golden brown. Serve alongside the spiced shallots and a salad, if desired.

2 FOR 1

BUY 4 LAMB CHOPS, COOK
THEM IN THE FIRST RECIPE,
AND USE THE LEFTOVERS IN
THE NEXT RECIPE.

Lamb Steaks
with rosemary cannellini beans

Lamb steaks are relatively cheap, but they can be just as tasty as beef steaks if treated with respect. In the first recipe, the beans take on the rosemary extremely well, and they can be mashed if you like, for a nice alternative to mashed potato. Since you've already done the hard work cooking the lamb, the salad in the second recipe is superspeedy, needing only that you add feta, arugula, and peppers.

2 x 8-oz [225-g] lamb steaks
Olive oil, for frying and drizzling
1 small onion, diced
2 garlic cloves, crushed
1 tsp dried rosemary
14-oz [400-g] can cannellini beans, rinsed and drained
⅞ to 1 cup [200 to 250 ml] water
Sea salt and freshly ground black pepper

Rub the steaks with olive oil and season with a generous amount of salt and pepper. Heat a frying pan over high heat and, when hot, add the steaks and sear for 2 minutes each side, or until well colored. Remove and set aside.

Pour away any excess oil from the pan, then add the onion, garlic, and rosemary and sweat over low heat until the onion is soft, about 5 minutes. Add the beans and ⅝ cup [150 ml] water. Simmer gently for 4 minutes. If the pan looks a bit dry, then add a little more water.

Add both lamb steaks to the pan along with any juices that have run off. Cover and cook for 4 to 6 minutes depending on the thickness of the meat and adding a little more water if the pan looks like it is boiling dry.

Remove the steaks to a plate and let them rest for a few minutes. Plate up half the beans and set aside the rest for the next recipe. Slice one of the steaks and rest on top of the plate of beans. Set aside the second steak for the next recipe. Add a drizzle of olive oil to the plate and serve with a fresh salad, if desired.

When the reserved lamb and beans have cooled, refrigerate them until ready to use in the second recipe.

Lamb and Feta Salad

1 leftover cooked lamb steak from recipe above
1 roasted red bell pepper from a jar, drained
¼ cup [35 g] crumbled feta
⅔ cup [100 g] leftover cooked beans from recipe above
2 handfuls of arugula

Dressing
1 Tbsp olive oil
Lemon juice, to taste
Sea salt and freshly ground black pepper

Bring the leftover lamb steak and beans to room temperature. Cut the lamb into thin slices. Do the same with the pepper. Mix together the ingredients for the dressing.

Combine the lamb, pepper, feta, beans, and arugula. Drizzle over the dressing and serve.

2 FOR 1

BUY 2 LAMB STEAKS, COOK THEM IN THE FIRST RECIPE, AND USE THE LEFTOVERS IN THE NEXT RECIPE.

BIG COOK

4 FOR 1

BUY 2 LAMB SHANKS, COOK THEM IN THE FIRST RECIPE, AND USE THE LEFTOVERS IN THE FOLLOWING RECIPES.

Slow-Cooked Lamb Shanks
with olives and polenta

Lamb shank, because it's on the bone, becomes ridiculously tender and tasty when slow-cooked. The sauce here has everything—sweetness, saltiness, richness, and piquancy. Two lunches and two dinners from one modest effort seems like a pretty good deal to me! So here we also have Lamb Pita; Stroganoff, and a great sandwich—not bad eh?!

2 lamb shanks (total weight about 1⅔ lb/750 g)
2 Tbsp all-purpose flour, seasoned with salt and pepper
Olive oil, for frying
1 onion, diced
3 garlic cloves, crushed
2 celery stalks, cut into ⅜-in [1-cm] thick slices
⅝ cup [150 ml] red wine
14-oz [400-g] can chopped tomatoes
1 tsp sugar
1 tsp dried oregano
1 Tbsp black olives, pitted
About ½ cup [60 g] quick-cook polenta or cornmeal
Small piece of butter
Salt and freshly ground black pepper

Preheat the oven to 325°F [170°C].

Coat the lamb shanks in the seasoned flour. Heat a little olive oil in a Dutch oven over medium-high heat, then brown the lamb shanks all over for a few minutes. Remove them from the dish and pour away some of the excess fat if it looks like there's a lot.

In the same dish, gently sweat the onion, garlic, and celery for 5 minutes. Add the wine and let bubble for 2 minutes. Add the tomatoes, sugar, and oregano, and season with salt and pepper. Simmer for 5 minutes. Now add the lamb shanks and bring to a boil. Reduce to a simmer and simmer for 1 hour 45 minutes to 2 hours until the meat falls off the bone.

Remove the lamb, and shred about three-quarters of the meat off one of the shanks. Keep in a warm place. Put the dish, with the sauce, over very low heat and add the olives. Simmer gently for 5 minutes. Prepare the polenta or cornmeal according to the package directions, then add the butter and plenty of of salt and pepper to taste.

Plate up the polenta, top with the shredded lamb, and then spoon over the sauce. Let the remaining lamb cool, then cover and refrigerate until ready to use in the next recipes.

Minty Lamb Sandwich

1¾ oz [50 g] leftover cooked lamb
  shank from recipe on page 123
½ Tbsp mayonnaise
1 tsp mint sauce
2 slices of bread, or a roll
Small handful of arugula

Cut the lamb into thin pieces. Combine the mayonnaise and mint sauce.
Spread over the bread and layer the lamb and arugula on top.

BIG COOK
LEFTOVERS

Lamb Stroganoff

Olive oil, for frying
1 small onion, diced
¼ tsp hot smoked paprika
5 white mushrooms
1¾ oz [50 g] leftover cooked
    lamb shank from recipe on
    page 123, torn
1½ Tbsp sour cream
Squeeze of lemon juice
Sea salt and freshly ground black
    pepper
Pasta or rice, to serve

Heat a little olive oil in a frying pan over low heat, then add the onion and paprika and sweat the onion for 5 minutes, or until soft but not colored. Slice the mushrooms and add to the pan. Cook for another 2 to 3 minutes. Add the lamb and continue to cook for 2 minutes.

Add the sour cream and cook for another 2 minutes. Squeeze over a good amount of lemon juice and season to taste with salt and pepper. Serve on pasta or rice.

Lamb, Feta, and Hummus Pita

1¾ oz [50 g] leftover cooked
   lamb shank from recipe on
   page 123, torn
1 pita bread
Hummus, to serve
¼ cup [35 g] crumbled feta
3 to 4 cherry tomatoes, halved

If you want the leftover lamb warm, reheat it in a frying pan with a little chicken broth over medium heat. Toast the pita. Slice to form a pocket (being careful, as they are the hottest things in the world!), spread with hummus, and fill with the torn lamb, feta, and tomatoes.

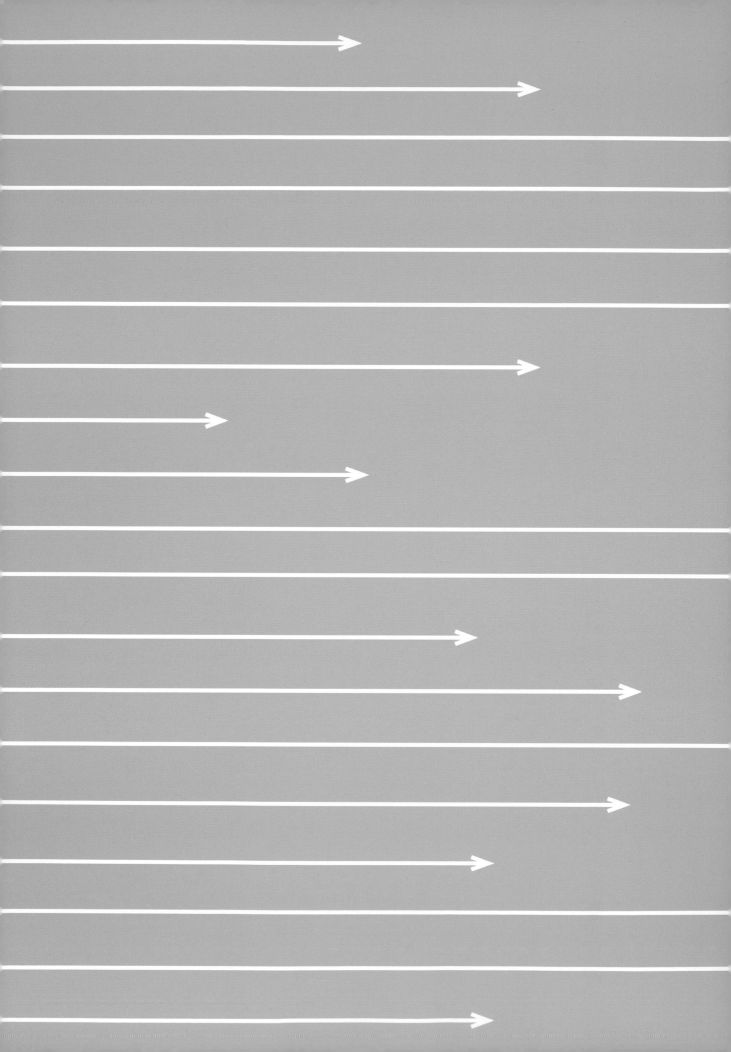

COD AND CHORIZO
WITH PESTO POTATOES AND PEAS

For the first recipe, any firm white fish similar to cod will work a treat. It's a lovely combo of flavors. And the fishcakes take leftovers to such a great place that you'll look for excuses to create leftovers all the time.

1 lb [500 g] new potatoes
Scant ½ cup [50 g] frozen peas
2¾ oz [75 g] chorizo
Olive oil, for frying
2 5¼ oz [150 g] cod fillets
2 tsp pesto
Sea salt and freshly ground black
    pepper

Boil the new potatoes in a saucepan of water until tender, about 15 minutes, adding the peas for a minute just before the end of the cooking time.

Meanwhile, skin the chorizo, cut it into quarters, and then cut it into ¼- to ⅜-in [½- to 1-cm] chunks. Rub olive oil all over the cod fillets and season them with salt and pepper.

Heat a little olive oil in a frying pan over medium heat and fry the chorizo for 2 minutes, or until golden brown. Remove the chorizo from the pan and set aside. In the same pan, cook the cod for 2 to 3 minutes each side, adding half the chorizo once you have cooked one side, or until the flesh starts to flake easily. If using cod with the skin on, cook it skin side down first.

Once the peas and potatoes are cooked, drain and set half the potatoes aside. To the rest of the potatoes and peas, mix through the pesto.

Plate up by spooning the pesto potatoes and peas in the center of a plate. Top with one of the fish fillets and surround with the hot chorizo. Add a drizzle more oil, if desired. Let the remaining fish fillet, chorizo, and potatoes cool, then cover and refrigerate for the next recipe.

2 FOR 1

BUY 2 COD FILLETS, COOK BOTH IN THE FIRST RECIPE, AND USE THE LEFTOVERS IN THE NEXT RECIPE.

CHORIZO FISHCAKES

*8¾ oz [250 g] leftover cooked new potatoes from recipe
  on page 130, peeled*
1 leftover cooked cod fillet from recipe on page 130
1 oz [30 g] leftover fried chorizo from recipe on page 130
Handful of fresh parsley (optional)
2 Tbsp all-purpose flour
1 egg, beaten
Couple of handfuls of bread crumbs
Olive oil, for frying
Sea salt and freshly ground black pepper

Mash the peeled new potatoes and flake in the cod.

Finely chop the chorizo and parsley, add to the potato mixture,
and combine. Season with salt and pepper. Shape into 2 to 3
patties. Dip each one in the flour, then the beaten egg and then
the bread crumbs.

Heat a glug of olive oil in a frying pan over medium heat, and fry
the fishcakes for 5 minutes each side, or until golden, crisp, and
piping hot.

QUICK SHRIMP CURRY

Shrimp take center stage in this pair of recipes. First up, there's a lovely mild, creamy curry with plenty of sauce (some of which could even be kept aside for an instant curry). This is followed by a delightfully crunchy, lemony shrimp and green bean salad—a perfect summer plate.

3½ oz [100 g] raw, shelled shrimp
1¼-in [3-cm] piece of ginger, peeled
1 garlic clove
1 red onion
1 red chile
1 Tbsp peanut oil
¾ Tbsp tikka masala paste
14-oz [400-g] can coconut milk
1 Tbsp tomato paste
Sea salt and freshly ground black pepper
Basmati rice, to serve
Fresh cilantro, to serve (optional)

Devein the shrimp by running a small, sharp knife down the back of them and pulling out the black vein.

Mince the ginger, garlic, onion, and chile either in a food processor, or by hand with a knife. Heat the peanut oil in a saucepan or frying pan over low heat, then add the chopped ginger mixture and the tikka masala paste and sweat for 5 minutes. Start preparing your rice at this point.

Add the coconut milk and tomato paste to the curry pan. Simmer for 10 minutes and add salt and pepper to taste. Add the shrimp and cook for a couple of minutes until they change color to pink and they are cooked through. Serve on your rice with cilantro, if desired.

2 FOR 1

BUY 7 OZ [200 G] RAW SHRIMP AND COOK HALF IN EACH RECIPE.

GRIDDLED SHRIMP WITH LEMONY GREEN BEAN SALAD

3½ oz [100 g] green beans, trimmed
Olive oil, for frying
3½ oz [100 g] raw, shelled shrimp
Boston lettuce, torn
1 shallot, thinly sliced
Sea salt and freshly ground black pepper

Dressing
1 tsp Dijon mustard
1 Tbsp lemon juice
2 Tbsp crème fraîche
Pinch of sugar

Boil or steam the green beans for a few minutes until they are tender but still have a crunch. Once cooked, run them under cold water to cool and preserve their vibrant color.

Mix together the ingredients for the dressing.

Devein the shrimp by running a small, sharp knife down the back of them and pulling out the black vein. Coat them in olive oil and season with salt and pepper. Put a griddle or frying pan over high heat and, once smoking hot (make sure your extractor fan is on), add the shrimp and cook for 45 seconds each side until they change color to pink and are cooked.

Chuck together the lettuce, shallot, and green beans. Coat in the dressing and top with the griddled shrimp.

SEAFOOD PAELLA

Use whatever seafood you can get your hands on to make this paella; I think shrimp and mussels work best. You can get handy bags of seafood that are great for no-fuss dinners like this. Leftover paella makes fantastically tasty rice balls—*arancini*. Oven-baking them (rather than deep-frying) keeps them healthier. Fill them with whatever you fancy, for example black olives stuffed with cheese.

Olive oil, for frying
1 onion, diced
1 garlic clove, crushed
1¾ oz [50 g] chorizo, sliced ⅜ in [1 cm] thick
¼ tsp paprika
⅔ cup [150 g] risotto rice
Splash of sherry (optional)
2 cups [500 ml] hot chicken broth
Couple of handfuls of your chosen seafood
Sea salt and freshly ground black pepper
Lemon wedge and fresh parsley, to serve

2 FOR 1

MAKE PAELLA RICE IN THE FIRST RECIPE AND USE THE LEFTOVERS IN THE NEXT RECIPE.

Heat 2 Tbsp olive oil in a large frying pan over low heat and gently sweat the onion and garlic for 5 minutes, or until soft but without color. Add the chorizo and paprika and cook for 2 minutes.

Add the rice, stirring to coat it in the oils in the pan. Then add a splash of sherry, if using, and cook it until most of it has evaporated. Add the broth, bit by bit, and let it be mostly absorbed before adding more. Keep simmering over gentle heat, stirring, until the broth has been used up and the rice is cooked through, about 15 minutes. Push the chorizo to one side and spoon half the rice into a separate container for the next recipe. Cool it quickly, then refrigerate until ready to use.

At this point, add your chosen seafood to the pan; it's best to cover the pan for this. Timings: cook deveined raw shrimp for a couple of minutes until pink; if the shrimp are ready-cooked, heat them until warmed through; cook mussels and clams until they are opened and discard any that don't open. Serve with a wedge of lemon and a scattering of parsley.

EASY ARANCINI

1 cup [175 g] chilled leftover paella from recipe above
3 cubes of mozzarella or cheddar, or 3 black olives, to fill (optional)
All-purpose flour, for dusting
1 egg, beaten
1 slice of bread, processed into bread crumbs, or 3 Tbsp bread crumbs

Preheat the oven to 400°F [200°C].

Put some wax paper on a baking sheet. (Stick it to the sheet with a smear of butter.)

Take the chilled leftover paella, divide it into 3 equal portions, and shape them into balls. At this point, you can push a cube of mozzarella or cheddar, or a black olive, into the center of the ball and reform the rice around it to cover it. Alternatively, you can leave the arancini plain. Dip each one in the flour, then the beaten egg, and then the bread crumbs.

Roast the arancini on the prepared baking sheet in the preheated oven for 20 to 25 minutes until golden brown and crisp. Serve with a side salad or a quick tomato sauce.

FAST FISH PIE

From start to plate, this fish pie takes 25 minutes max! The bread crumb crust is a triumph with its blend of lemon, herb, and garlic. And it's this crust that packs so much flavor power into your follow-up fishcakes. The quantity of fish needed isn't critical, so a little more will do no harm. If you serve the pie with some boiled new potatoes, make extra and use those leftover potatoes for your fishcakes. Both recipes go well with tomato and shallot salad.

1 Tbsp [15 g] butter, plus extra for
  greasing
2 x 4 oz [110 g] white fish fillets
  (I used haddock)
Juice and grated zest of ½ lemon
1¾ oz [50 g] white, crust-free bread
1 fat garlic clove
2 Tbsp fresh parsley
Drizzle of olive oil
Sea salt and freshly ground black
  pepper

Preheat the oven to 400°F [200°C].

Grease a baking dish and place the fish fillets inside it. Season it with salt and pepper and drizzle over the lemon juice.

Blitz together the lemon zest, bread, garlic, parsley, butter, and oil in a food processor until it forms fine, fragrant bread crumbs. Sprinkle this evenly over the fish fillets. Bake, uncovered, in the preheated oven for 15 to 20 minutes, depending on thickness, until cooked through. Plate up one portion of fast fish pie, with a tomato and shallot salad, green beans, or boiled new potatoes. Let the remaining portion of fish cool, then cover and refrigerate until ready to use in the next recipe.

10 MINUTE FISHCAKES

*Leftover fast fish pie from
  recipe left*
*9 oz [250 g] new potatoes,
  boiled and mashed*
2 Tbsp all-purpose flour
1 egg, beaten
*Couple of handfuls of
  bread crumbs*
Olive oil, for frying
*Sea salt and freshly ground
  black pepper*

Flake the leftover fast fish pie (including the topping) and mix it together with the potatoes. Season with salt and pepper. Form into 2 patties. Dip each one in the flour, then the beaten egg, and then the bread crumbs.

Heat a glug of olive oil in a frying pan over medium heat, and fry the fishcakes for 5 minutes each side, or until golden, crisp, and piping hot.

2 FOR 1

COOK TWO 4 OZ [110 G] WHITE FISH FILLETS IN THE FIRST RECIPE AND USE THE LEFTOVERS IN THE NEXT.

MUSSELS IN BEER

This is a lovely alternative to the classic *moules marinières* using lager instead of wine and giving a darker but sweet flavor. The linguine in the second recipe is a dish I first had at a beach café in Corsica and, even if you've never been there, this great combo of ingredients will transport you there, too. Pure sunshine!

2¼ lb [1 kg] mussels
2 shallots
2 garlic cloves
Small piece of butter
1 bottle of light lager (I use Beck's)
1 Tbsp cream
Squeeze of lemon juice
Freshly ground black pepper
Crusty bread or French fries,
   to serve

Wash the mussels thoroughly and "debeard" them by pulling the hairy "beards" off the shells. Discard any cracked or open mussels.

Dice the shallots and crush the garlic. Melt the butter in a large saucepan over medium heat, then sweat the shallots and garlic for 5 minutes, or until soft but with no color. Add the lager and bring to a boil.

Now add the mussels, cover, and cook, shaking the pan regularly, for a few minutes until all the mussels have opened.

Remove the mussels with a slotted spoon (keeping the cooking liquor in the pan) and place half in a bowl. Set the remaining mussels aside to cool, then extract them from their shells and refrigerate until ready to use in the next recipe.

Add the cream and lemon juice to the cooking liquor and simmer for a minute or so. Season with black pepper, stir, and pour over the mussels in the bowl. Serve with crusty bread or French fries.

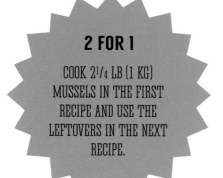

2 FOR 1

COOK 2¹/₄ LB [1 KG]
MUSSELS IN THE FIRST
RECIPE AND USE THE
LEFTOVERS IN THE NEXT
RECIPE.

MUSSEL LINGUINE

Olive oil, for frying
2 garlic cloves, crushed
14-oz [400-g] can chopped
   tomatoes
Pinch of sugar
1 tsp dried red pepper flakes
1 tsp capers (optional)
3½ oz [100 g] leftover cooked,
   shelled mussels from recipe
   above
3½ oz [100 g] linguine
Sea salt and freshly ground black
   pepper
Fresh parsley, to serve

Put a saucepan of water on for your pasta.

Heat a glug of olive oil in a saucepan over gentle heat, then sweat the garlic for 2 minutes. Add the tomatoes, sugar, red pepper flakes, and capers, if using, and simmer very gently for 10 to 15 minutes. Season with salt and pepper to taste.

Cook the pasta in the pan of boiling water when the time is right.

When the pasta is almost ready, tip the mussels into the tomato sauce and warm through very gently for a minute or two, making sure they don't toughen up. Check the seasoning again.

Plate up your pasta in a large bowl and top with the sauce and a sprinkling of fresh parsley.

SMOKED MACKEREL PATE WITH A KICK

Very healthy, this—and easy; straight out of the package! All you need is a fork, a bowl, and a spoon. The Niçoise that follows has been updated to replace the usual tuna (expensive) with mackerel (sustainable), making something of equal delight ...

1 smoked mackerel fillet
1½ Tbsp thick Greek yogurt
1 tsp horseradish sauce
Lemon juice, to taste
Sea salt and freshly ground black pepper
Crackers, crispbreads, or toast, to serve

Peel the skin off the mackerel, then flake the flesh into a bowl. Add the yogurt and horseradish sauce, and mash and mix with a fork. Add the lemon juice, salt, and pepper to taste. Serve chilled on anything crunchy such as crackers, crispbreads, or really good toast.

2 FOR 1

BUY 2 SMOKED MACKEREL FILLETS AND USE ONE IN EACH RECIPE.

SMOKED MACKEREL NICOISE

7 oz [200 g] new potatoes
1½ oz [40 g] green beans, trimmed
1 smoked mackerel fillet
1 Tbsp black olives
3 cherry tomatoes, chopped
Boston lettuce, torn
Handful of croutons

Dressing
½ tsp sugar
½ tsp Dijon mustard
1 Tbsp lemon juice
3 Tbsp extra virgin olive oil

Boil the new potatoes in a saucepan of water, adding the green beans when the potatoes are starting to soften. Once everything is cooked, whip out the green beans and run them under cold water to cool and preserve their vibrant color.

Meanwhile, combine the ingredients for the dressing. Peel the skin off the mackerel, then flake the flesh. Pit the olives.

Put the potatoes, beans, tomatoes, olives, and lettuce in a bowl. Coat in the dressing and top with the flaked mackerel and croutons.

NORDIC SMOKED SALMON WRAP

Smoked salmon is one of those foods that lends itself to quick cooking. The wrap recipe is pure and simple, relying on the high quality of the ingredients; and the pasta in the second recipe is wonderfully creamy, smoky, and fresh. Superspeedy; maximum effect.

1 Tbsp crème fraîche or cream cheese
1 wrap, such as tortilla wrap
2 slices of smoked salmon (about 1 oz/30 g offcuts)
1 small avocado, peeled, pitted, and sliced
2 cherry tomatoes, chopped
Squeeze of lemon juice
Sea salt and freshly ground black pepper

Spread the crème fraîche or cream cheese over the wrap. Top with the smoked salmon, sliced avocado, chopped tomatoes, and lemon juice, and season with salt and pepper. Wrap up, cut in half, and enjoy.

2 FOR 1

BUY A SMALL PACKAGE OF SMOKED SALMON AND USE HALF IN EACH RECIPE.

CREAMY SMOKED SALMON PASTA

3½ oz [100 g] linguine
Handful of peas (optional)
2 Tbsp crème fraîche or cream cheese
1½ Tbsp lemon juice
1 tsp fresh dill, torn
2 slices of smoked salmon (about 1 oz/30 g offcuts)
Sea salt and freshly ground black pepper

Cook your linguine according to the package directions. If using peas, stick them in with the pasta 1 minute before it is ready.

Mix together the crème fraîche or cream cheese, lemon juice, and dill, and season well with pepper. Chop the salmon into bite-size pieces.

Once the pasta is cooked, drain it, and put it back in the pan with the creamy mixture. Stir well and let warm through for a minute. Serve in a large bowl and top with the smoked salmon.

SALMON PACKAGES

Due credit to my dad for coming up with the idea of adding the horseradish to these little steamed packages. It cuts beautifully across the rich oils of the salmon. The subsequent salmon pâté couldn't be easier and makes a great light lunch or snack.

7 oz [200 g] new potatoes, scrubbed
   clean
2 salmon fillets, about 4 oz [110 g]
   each
4 tsp horseradish sauce
10 thin slices of peeled cucumber
Small piece of butter
1 to 2 tsp torn fresh parsley
   and/or dill
Sea salt and freshly ground black
   pepper

Preheat the oven to 400°F [200°C].

Cut any large new potatoes in half, then boil or steam them for about 15 to 20 minutes until cooked through.

Meanwhile, place both salmon fillets on a sheet of foil or parchment paper in the center of a baking sheet. Season with salt and pepper, then spread the horseradish over them with a knife. Top with the cucumber slices. Pull up the sides of the foil or paper and fold over to seal the salmon in. Cook for 12 to 15 minutes, or until the salmon flakes easily.

Drain the cooked potatoes and toss them with the butter, parsley, or dill, and some salt and pepper. Serve with one of the salmon fillets. (This also goes brilliantly with a side salad or green beans.) Let the other salmon fillet cool, then refrigerate until ready to use.

SIMPLE SALMON PATE

1 leftover cooked salmon fillet from
   recipe left, skinned
½ Tbsp lemon juice
2 Tbsp crème fraîche or cream
   cheese
Sea salt and freshly ground black
   pepper

Flake the cooked salmon fillet with a fork, then place it in a bowl with the other ingredients. Mash and mix with the fork until well combined. Taste and adjust the seasoning. Serve on hot buttered toast or crackers.

2 FOR 1

BUY 2 SALMON FILLETS, COOK BOTH IN THE FIRST RECIPE, AND USE THE LEFTOVERS IN THE NEXT RECIPE.

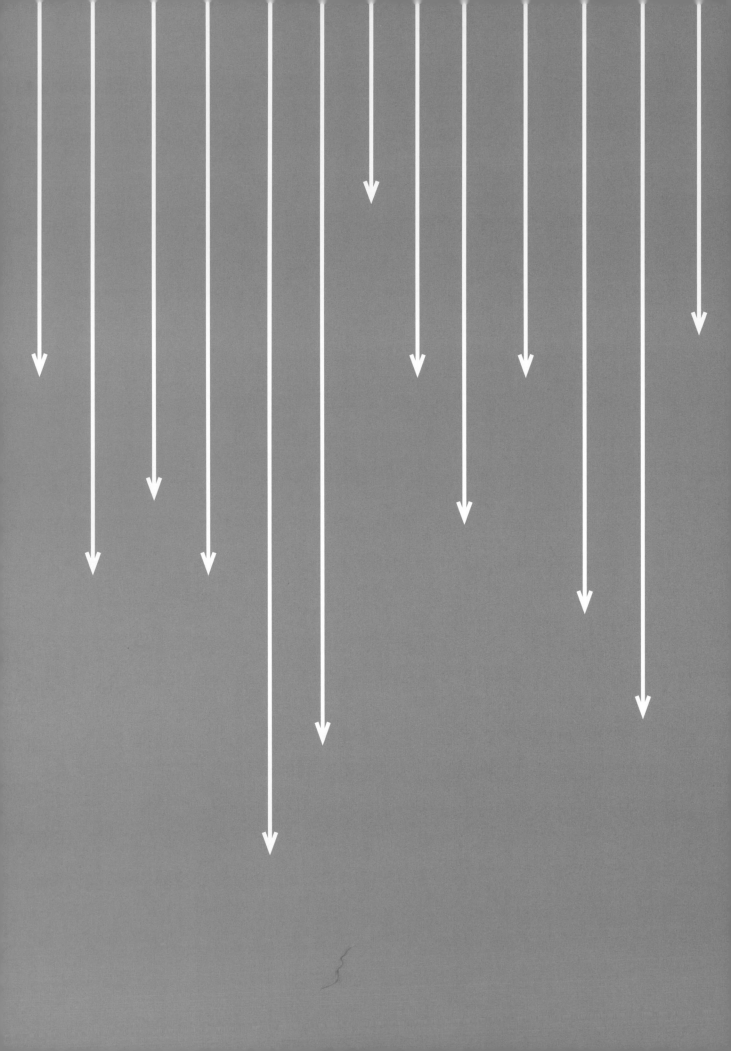

COOK

VEGETABLES

ROAST BUTTERNUT SQUASH
WITH RICOTTA AND ARUGULA ON GNOCCHI

You get a lot for your money with a butternut squash. It has a distinctive creamy flavor that works equally well on pasta and gnocchi—as well as making a delightfully addictive dip.

1¼ lb [600 g] butternut squash,
    peeled and seeded
1 Tbsp olive oil
2 tsp dried thyme
5¼ oz [150 g] gnocchi
1 Tbsp ricotta
Squeeze of lemon juice
Handful of arugula
Sea salt and freshly ground
    black pepper

Preheat the oven to 400°F [200°C].

Cut the butternut squash into ¾-in [2-cm] cubes. Place into a freezer bag with the olive oil, thyme, and some salt and pepper. Seal the bag and shake it to give the squash an even coating and then tip it out of the bag and onto a large baking sheet. Cook in the preheated oven for 20 minutes, or until soft and a pale golden color.

Meanwhile, put a saucepan of water onto boil for the gnocchi, then cook according to the package directions. Drain the gnocchi and return to the dry pan with the ricotta and lemon juice, half the cooked butternut squash, and some black pepper. Tip into a bowl and top with arugula and little olive oil. Let the rest of the butternut squash cool, cover, and refrigerate until ready to use in the next recipe.

2 FOR 1

BUY A BUTTERNUT SQUASH,
COOK IT IN THE FIRST RECIPE,
AND USE THE LEFTOVERS IN
THE NEXT RECIPE.

ROAST BUTTERNUT
SQUASH DIP

7 oz [200 g] leftover cooked
    butternut squash from
    recipe above
Scant ½ cup [100 g] ricotta
Squeeze of lemon juice
Freshly ground black pepper

Using a food processor or hand blender, blend together the cooked butternut squash, ricotta, lemon juice, and black pepper to taste. Let chill in the refrigerator until ready to use. Serve with crispbreads, hot crusty bread, or alongside a deli plate.

CREAMY LEEK AND PEAS
ON WARM CIABATTA

This fancy toast makes a lovely lunch. Bacon is an optional extra, but it does add a complementary dimension to the leek and peas. You can also make this as a side dish for a steak. The Glamorgan sausage recipe uses up any leftover leek and pea mixture. The sausages can be kept in the refrigerator once shaped, so you can prep them ahead of time if desired. There's even enough for two meals!

10½ oz [300 g] leek
2 slices of lean bacon (optional)
Olive oil, for frying
Splash of water
1 ciabatta roll
Scant 1 cup [100 g] frozen peas
Good squeeze of lemon juice
2 Tbsp crème fraîche
Sea salt and freshly ground black
    pepper

Thinly slice the leek into ¼-in [½-cm] thick circles. Cut the bacon, if using, into similar-size pieces. Heat a little olive oil in a saucepan over medium heat and fry the bacon for 3 to 4 minutes until the fat begins to run. Add the leek, stir, then add the water. Cover and gently cook for around 10 minutes, stirring occasionally, until the leek is nice and soft.

Meanwhile, cut the ciabatta through the middle, then toast, broil, or bake it lightly to warm it. To the leek mixture, add the peas and cook for 1 to 2 minutes. Remove from the heat, season with salt and pepper to taste, and add the lemon juice. Stir in the crème fraîche. Spoon half of the mixture onto the warm ciabatta and top with a little more black pepper and lemon juice. Let the remaining leek mixture cool, then cover and refrigerate it until ready to use in the next recipe.

2 FOR 1

BUY A LEEK AND FROZEN PEAS, COOK THEM IN THE FIRST RECIPE, AND USE THE LEFTOVERS IN THE NEXT RECIPE.

LEEK AND PEA
GLAMORGAN SAUSAGES

10½ oz [300 g] leftover leek
    mixture from recipe above
Scant ½ cup [50 g] grated
    sharp cheddar
1 tsp English mustard
Scant 1 cup [100 g] bread
    crumbs

Preheat the oven to 400°F [200°C]. Line a baking sheet with a sheet of parchment paper.

Combine the leek mixture, grated cheddar, mustard, and three-quarters of the bread crumbs. Shape and squeeze everything into 4 or 5 rough sausage shapes. Put the remaining bread crumbs on a plate, then dip and roll the sausages in them to get an even coating.

Place the sausages on the prepared baking sheet and cook in the preheated oven for 15 to 20 minutes until golden brown. Let sit for a moment and then carefully remove using a spatula. Serve with a tomato salad and a good dollop of apple chutney.

THAI LENTIL DHAL

A variation on the usual Indian dhal, my version is inspired by Thai flavors. It's one of the thriftiest dinners you can make—but it tastes well above its class. The pâté is one of my all-time favorites and also happens to be ridiculously easy to make.

1 Tbsp peanut oil
2 garlic cloves, crushed
1 onion, diced
3 tsp Thai red curry paste (if you are veggie, check the packaging, as a lot of pastes include shrimp or fish sauce)
¾ cup [160 g] red split lentils, washed
2 tsp tomato paste
14 oz [400-g] can coconut milk
7 Tbsp [100 ml] water
Juice of ½ lemon
Sea salt and freshly ground black pepper
Naan bread and chapatis, to serve

Heat the peanut oil in a large saucepan over very gentle heat, then sweat the garlic and onion for 5 minutes, or until soft and translucent. Add the curry paste, stir, and cook for another minute.

Add the lentils, tomato paste, coconut milk, and water. Bring to a boil and simmer for 20 minutes, stirring regularly. Remove from the heat, add the lemon juice, taste, and season to taste with salt and pepper.

Plate up half the dhal and serve with naan bread or chapatis, or as an accompaniment to other curries. Let the other half of the dhal cool, then refrigerate until ready to use in the following recipe.

2 FOR 1

MAKE A RED-LENTIL DHAL IN THE FIRST RECIPE, THEN USE THE LEFTOVERS IN THE NEXT RECIPE.

LENTIL, COCONUT, AND CILANTRO PATE

10½ oz [300 g] leftover Thai Lentil Dhal from recipe above
1 large handful of fresh cilantro
Sea salt and freshly ground black pepper
Lemon juice (optional)
Warm toast or crispbreads, to serve

Using a food processor or hand blender, blitz the leftover Thai Lentil Dhal with the cilantro until you have a nice smooth pâté with specks of green. Taste and season with salt and pepper, and lemon juice, if desired.

Let chill in the refrigerator until ready to use. Serve with warm toast or crispbreads.

EGGPLANT AND TOMATO FUSILLI

One eggplant; two dishes! Eggplant has a special place in the kitchen for its unique capacity to absorb flavors—in this case some piquant numbers. This is followed by a salad featuring the deep and earthy taste of miso.

3½ oz [100 g] eggplant
3 cherry tomatoes
Small handful of fresh basil
3½ oz [100 g] fusilli
1½ tsp red wine vinegar
½ shallot, diced
1 Tbsp olive oil, plus extra
    for frying
Squeeze of lemon juice
Sea salt and freshly ground black
    pepper
Parmesan shavings, to serve

Put a large saucepan of salted water onto boil for the fusilli.

Meanwhile, chop the eggplant into ⅝-in [1.5-cm] cubes. Cut the tomatoes into quarters. Tear the basil. Combine the red wine vinegar, shallot, and the 1 Tbsp olive oil in a bowl.

Cook the pasta according to the package directions. Coat the eggplant lightly in olive oil and fry in a frying pan over medium heat for about 5 minutes until golden and cooked through. Remove from the pan, squeeze over the lemon juice, and season with salt and pepper.

Drain the cooked pasta and return it to the pan. Add the eggplant, tomatoes, basil, and the vinegar mixture. Combine well and check for seasoning. Plate up, top with Parmesan shavings, and squeeze over a little more lemon juice, to taste.

2 FOR 1

BUY ONE EGGPLANT, COOK PART OF IT IN THE FIRST RECIPE, AND USE THE REST IN THE NEXT RECIPE.

MISO EGGPLANT SALAD

7 oz [200 g] eggplant
1 Tbsp peanut oil
2 tsp brown miso paste
2 tsp rice wine
2 tsp rice wine vinegar
1 Boston lettuce, leaves separated
2 scallions, finely chopped
Toasted sesame oil, for dressing

Cut the eggplant into ⅝-in [1.5-cm] wide strips. Toss it in the peanut oil. Fry it in a saucepan over medium heat for about 5 minutes, or until golden brown.

Meanwhile, combine the miso paste, rice wine, and rice wine vinegar in a bowl.

Once the eggplant is soft and well colored, remove from the heat, add the miso mixture, and toss to combine.

Place the leaves in a bowl, top with the eggplant and scallions, and finally drizzle with sesame oil.

SPICY GARBANZO AND POTATO SOUP

Here again, cheap ingredients are transformed in the company of harissa, a spice paste widely used in North Africa and the Middle East and which is made from chile and a mix of over 40 herbs and spices. The Lebanese salad in second place is incredibly healthy and a real doddle!

Olive oil, for frying
1 onion, diced
7 oz [200 g] potato, peeled
Scant ¾ cup [120 g] garbanzo beans (chickpeas) (half a 14-oz/400-g can, drained)
1 to 2 tsp rose harissa paste (quantity depends on heat required)
2 cups [500 ml] vegetable broth
Sea salt and freshly ground black pepper

Heat a glug of olive oil in a saucepan over gentle heat, then sweat the onion for about 5 minutes, or until translucent. Meanwhile, chop the potato into ⅜-in [1-cm] chunks.

Add the potato, drained garbanzo beans, harissa paste, and broth to the pan. Bring to a boil, then simmer for 8 to 10 minutes, or until the potato is soft.

Remove the pan from the heat and blend with a hand blender (or let cool slightly and use a blender or food processor) until very smooth. Season to taste.

2 FOR 1

BUY A 14-OZ [400-G] CAN OF GARBANZO BEANS (CHICKPEAS) AND USE HALF IN EACH RECIPE.

LEBANESE-STYLE GARBANZO SALAD

¾-in [2-cm] piece of cucumber
2 cherry tomatoes
1 Tbsp lemon juice
1 Tbsp olive oil
1½ Tbsp each chopped fresh cilantro and parsley
Scant ¾ cup [120 g] garbanzo beans (chickpeas) (half a 14-oz/400-g can, drained)
Sea salt and freshly ground black pepper

Peel and dice the cucumber. Dice the tomatoes. Combine the lemon juice, olive oil, and herbs in a bowl. Add the garbanzo beans, tomatoes, and cucumber, combine, and season well with salt and pepper.

VEGGIE FAJITAS

You can, of course, play about with the fillings for these fajitas. Peppers, refried beans, onions, zucchini, mushrooms—it's your choice! The Mexican salad is my sister's favorite thing (hardly surprising since it's so good). Be warned; you will want more …

1 eggplant
2 tsp rose harissa paste
2 Tbsp olive oil
Squeeze of lemon juice
1 to 2 tortilla wraps
1 to 2 Tbsp sour cream or crème fraîche
½ avocado, sliced
A little lettuce (optional)
Small handful of fresh cilantro
Sea salt and freshly ground black pepper

Slice the eggplant into ⅛-in [¼-cm] thick circles or half-circles. Combine the harissa and olive oil in a bowl and add the eggplant. Stir to coat well. Heat a griddle pan over high heat until smoking. Quickly season the eggplant with salt and pepper and add it to the hot griddle pan in batches so as not to overcrowd the pan. Cook for 1 minute each side, or until nicely charred. Remove to a plate, squeeze over a little lemon juice, and cook the remaining eggplant in the same way.

Assemble the fajita: start with the sour cream or crème fraîche, top with half of the eggplant, the avocado, cilantro, and a little lettuce. Roll up and get stuck in. Let the leftover eggplant cool, then cover and refrigerate until ready to use in the next recipe.

2 FOR 1

BUY 1 EGGPLANT AND 1 AVOCADO, USE SOME IN THE FIRST RECIPE, THEN USE THE LEFTOVERS IN THE NEXT RECIPE.

MEXICAN SALAD

Leftover cooked harissa eggplant from recipe above
Large handful of lightly salted tortilla chips
½ avocado, sliced
2 small tomatoes, cut into eighths
Small handful of fresh cilantro
1 Boston lettuce, torn
Scant ¼ cup [25 g] grated cheddar cheese

Dressing
2 Tbsp olive oil
2 tsp balsamic vinegar
1 tsp honey
1 tsp ketchup
Small pinch of sea salt

Combine the ingredients for the dressing.

In a large bowl, mix the leftover harissa eggplant, the tortilla chips, avocado, tomatoes, cilantro, lettuce, and grated cheddar. Top with the dressing and mix with your hands to get an even coating. Tip into a serving dish and you're done!

TOFU AND CUCUMBER SALAD

Tofu is a great receptor of flavor, and this recipe has lots of it. It's a very refreshing, Chinese-inspired dish. The second recipe makes a great, quick appetizer or can be served with noodles and veg for an exotic main.

1 Tbsp light soy sauce
2 tsp toasted sesame oil
8 oz [225 g] firm tofu (half a pack), drained and cut into bite-size chunks
2-in [5-cm] piece of cucumber, cut lengthwise into ribbons with a mandolin or vegetable peeler
1 scallion, shredded
Small handful of fresh cilantro, torn

Combine the soy sauce and sesame oil in a bowl. Pat the tofu dry with paper towels.

Put the cucumber in a shallow bowl and top with the tofu, scallion, and cilantro. Drizzle with the soy sauce dressing.

2 FOR 1

BUY A 14³/₄-OZ [450-G] PACK OF FIRM TOFU AND USE HALF IN EACH RECIPE.

SALT 'N' PEPPER TOFU

8 oz [225 g] firm tofu (half a pack), drained and cut into
  bite-size chunks
½ tsp coarse sea salt
½ tsp sugar
¾ tsp whole Szechuan peppercorns
½ Tbsp all-purpose flour
1 tsp toasted sesame oil
1 shallot, very thinly sliced
Peanut oil, for frying
Egg noodles, to serve

Pat the tofu dry with paper towels. Crush the sea salt, sugar, and Szechuan peppercorns with a mortar and pestle or a spice grinder until it becomes a fine powder. Mix the powder with the flour. Dip the tofu chunks in this powder until evenly coated.

Heat a good glug of oil in a frying pan over medium-high heat. Fry the tofu for about 1 minute each side, or until golden brown. Meanwhile, heat the sesame oil in a separate pan and fry the shallot until crispy.

Serve the tofu and shallot with egg noodles.

GRIDDLED SCALLION TART

This lovely duo of thrifty Mediterranean tarts makes use of quick and easy ready-made puff pastry. The fresh flavors here make for a delightful light lunch or supper—and served with a salad, you can easily get a couple of portions out of each.

6 scallions
Olive oil, for frying
5¾ oz [160 g] all-butter puff pastry
    (half a 11¼-oz/320-g pack)
½ cup [75 g] crumbled feta
½ to 1 Tbsp chopped fresh mint
Freshly ground black pepper

Preheat the oven to 425°F [220°C].

Heat a griddle pan over high heat until smoking (make sure your extractor fan is on). Trim the scallions and coat with a little olive oil. Put the scallions on the hot griddle pan to cook for 2 minutes each side, or until they have a nice char. Remove the pan from the heat and set the scallions aside.

Using a rolling pin, roll out the puff pastry on a lightly floured board to a rectangle about ⅛ to ⅙ in [3 to 4 mm] thick. Place on a baking sheet and top with the crumbled feta. Arrange the scallions on top, sprinkle over the mint, and season well with pepper. Add a final drizzle of olive oil if desired.

Bake in the preheated oven for 10 to 12 minutes, or until golden brown, puffed up, and cooked through. Serve with a side salad.

2 FOR 1

BUY A 11¼-OZ [320-G] PACK OF PUFF PASTRY AND USE HALF IN EACH RECIPE.

ARTICHOKE HEART, BASIL, AND MOZZARELLA TART

2¾ oz [75 g] mozzarella
3½ oz [100 g] artichoke hearts in a jar, drained of oil
5¾ oz [160 g] all-butter puff pastry
*   (half a 11¼-oz/320-g pack)*
1 Tbsp fresh basil leaves, torn
Sea salt and freshly ground black pepper
Olive oil, for frying

Preheat the oven to 425°F [220°C].

Thinly slice the mozzarella and coarsely chop the drained artichoke hearts.

Using a rolling pin, roll out the puff pastry on a lightly floured board to a rectangle about ⅛ to ⅙ in [3 to 4 mm] thick. Place on a baking sheet and top evenly with the mozzarella, then add the artichoke hearts, basil, salt and pepper, and a drizzle of olive oil.

Bake in the preheated oven for 10 to 12 minutes, or until golden brown, puffed up, and cooked through. Finish with a little more basil and serve with a tomato and red onion salad.

RATATOUILLE

In this tasty duo of recipes, strong ingredients combine to make wonderfully rich flavors. I particularly like the piquancy from the capers and olives. Everything works really well when transformed into the soup, served minestrone-style. Bellissimo!

1 eggplant
1 zucchini
Olive oil, for frying
1 small onion, diced
14-oz [400-g] can chopped tomatoes
½ Tbsp balsamic vinegar
1 tsp capers
½ Tbsp black olives, pitted
2 pinches of dried thyme
Sea salt and freshly ground black pepper

Cut the eggplant and zucchini into quarters, lengthwise, then cut into bite-size chunks. Stick these into a bowl and drizzle with olive oil and a little salt and pepper. Mix well until they have an even coating.

Put a frying pan over high heat and cook the eggplant and zucchini for 3 to 4 minutes until golden brown. You may want to cook them in batches to avoid overcrowding the pan. Remove to a plate and set aside.

Heat a glug of olive oil in the same pan over gentle heat and sweat the onion for about 5 minutes until soft and translucent. Add the tomatoes, balsamic vinegar, capers, olives, and thyme and simmer gently for about 5 minutes.

Add the eggplant and zucchini, cover, and simmer gently for about 10 minutes, or until soft. Taste and adjust the seasoning; remember that the olives and capers provide salty bursts, so you might not need to add much.

Plate up half the ratatouille and serve with lovely crusty bread or as a side dish to a roast or any bits you fancy. It also makes a cracking filling for a sandwich, hot or cold. Keep the other half for the next recipe, which you can start straightaway or let cool, then cover and refrigerate.

2 FOR 1

MAKE A BIG PORTION OF RATATOUILLE IN THE FIRST RECIPE AND USE THE LEFTOVERS IN THE NEXT RECIPE.

RATATOUILLE AND PASTA SOUP

1¾ oz [50 g] macaroni pasta
10½ oz [300 g] leftover ratatouille from recipe on page 166
About ⅞ cup [200 ml] vegetable broth
Olive oil, for drizzling

Put a saucepan of salted water onto boil for the pasta. Cook according to the package directions, then drain.

Meanwhile, blend half the leftover ratatouille mix in a blender or food processor until smooth. Tip into a saucepan with the vegetable broth and the remaining ratatouille. Add a little more broth if you like a thinner soup. Heat, stirring occasionally, until piping hot. Add the pasta just before serving, and drizzle a little olive oil on top.

PASTA WITH ROASTED PEPPERS AND GOAT CHEESE

Roasted bell peppers from a jar are fantastic and they take out all the fuss and faff so you can create these delicious dishes in no time. The pasta dish is rich, creamy but fresh, and the Turkish pizza is based on a clever, foolproof dough that provides a lovely contrast to this gorgeous topping.

3½ oz [100 g] pasta of your choice
Olive oil, for frying
1 small onion, diced
1 garlic clove, crushed
1¾ oz [50 g] roasted red bell peppers
    from a jar, drained
1 oz [25 g] goat cheese
Squeeze of lemon juice
Sea salt and freshly ground black
    pepper

Put a saucepan of cold water, with a dash of salt, onto boil for the pasta. Cook the pasta according to the package directions to coincide with the timings for the sauce.

Heat a glug of olive oil in a saucepan over gentle heat, then sweat the onion and garlic for 5 minutes, or until soft and translucent. Coarsely chop the roasted red bell peppers, add to the pan, and cook for another 1 to 2 minutes.

Blitz the contents of the pan with a hand blender, or transfer to a food processor and blitz until smooth. Add the goat cheese and blitz again until smooth. Season with salt and pepper to taste.

Once the pasta has cooked, drain, and then fold in the sauce. Finish with a squeeze of lemon juice and more black pepper.

2 FOR 1

BUY A JAR OF ROASTED RED BELL PEPPERS AND USE SOME IN EACH RECIPE.

FAST TURKISH PIZZA

½ cup, plus 2 Tbsp [75 g] all-purpose flour, sifted
¼ cup [60 ml] plain yogurt
Handful of minced fresh basil
Pinch of sea salt

Topping
Olive oil
Handful of roasted red bell peppers from a jar, drained and sliced
Handful of crumbled goat cheese
A few thin slices of red onion

Other optional toppings
Tomato, olives, feta, pine nuts, artichoke hearts, cilantro, parsley,
   or any antipasti you can think of!

Preheat the broiler.

Combine the flour, yogurt, basil, and salt in a large bowl. Mix with your hands until it comes together into a dough. Divide into 2 balls and, using a rolling pin, roll each into very thin circles on a floured board.

Heat a dry frying pan until hot, then add one dough base and cook for 1 to 2 minutes each side until browned. Repeat with the other base. Drizzle each with a little olive oil. Top with the red peppers, goat cheese, red onion, and a little more oil. Stick under the broiler for a few minutes until the cheese has melted and starts to brown, but watch that the dough doesn't burn.

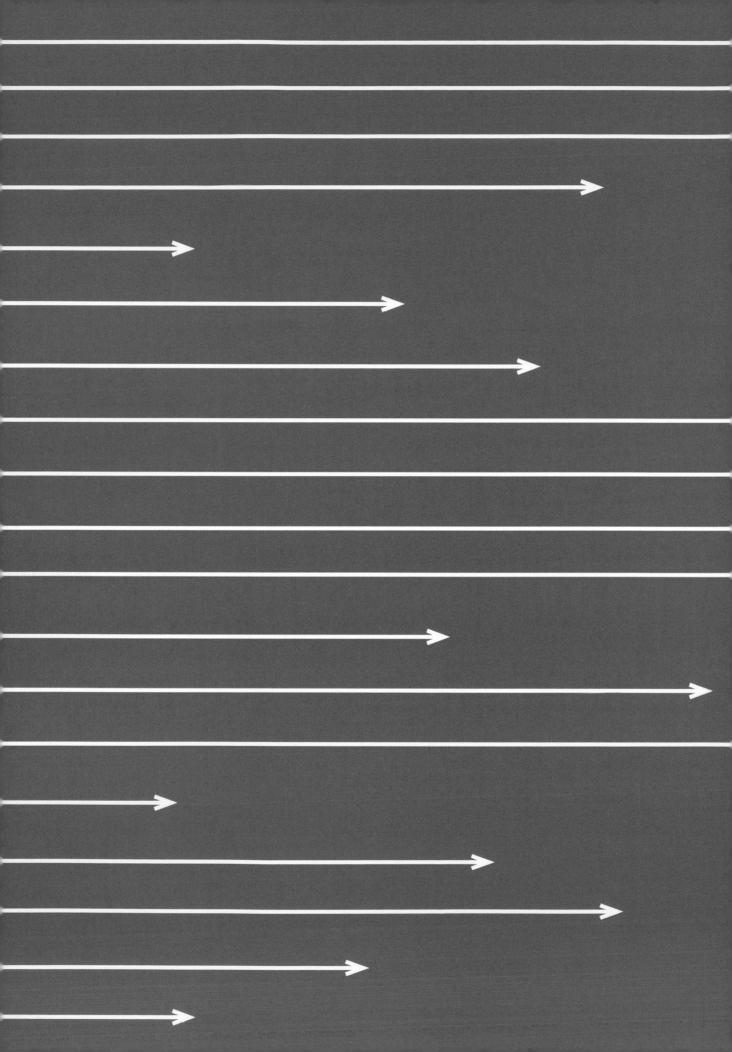

SWEET

TREATS

POPCORN

Popcorn can actually be very healthy—if you avoid adding sugary toppings! These are my versions of the going-to-the-movie theater classics of sweet and salty. Not especially healthy, but great fun to make and eat, and wonderfully tasty and indulgent.

2 Tbsp [25 g] popcorn kernels
Peanut oil

Add enough peanut oil to coat the bottom of a large, heavy-bottom saucepan. Place over medium-high heat and add the popcorn. Cover with a lid and cook, shaking the pan regularly, until the popping stops!

STICKY TOFFEE

1 Tbsp [15 g] brown sugar
1 Tbsp [15 g] butter
2 tsp light corn syrup

Make a batch of popcorn following the directions above.

Mix the sugar, butter, and corn syrup together in a saucepan and melt over gentle heat. Boil gently for 1 to 2 minutes, then pour over the hot popcorn.

PECORINO

1 Tbsp [15 g] butter, melted
1 Tbsp [10 g] finely grated
*   pecorino cheese*

Make a batch of popcorn following the directions above.

Toss the hot popcorn in the melted butter, then stir in the grated pecorino cheese.

COOKIE ROLLS

Yes—instant cookies! Keep the dough in the refrigerator for a week or more (or even longer in the freezer), and cut off and bake a slice whenever you yearn for that freshly baked cookie.

1 cup [225 g] salted butter, softened
1 cup [200 g] firmly packed soft
    brown sugar
½ cup [100 g] superfine sugar
1 tsp vanilla extract
2 large eggs, beaten
1½ cups [175 g] all-purpose flour
1 level tsp baking soda
1 tsp salt
4¼ oz [125 g] milk chocolate, finely
    chopped, or chocolate chips
½ cup [75 g] raisins
2½ cups [200 g] rolled oats

Cream together the butter and both sugars in a mixing bowl using a wooden spoon or electric beater until the mixture becomes light and fluffy. Add the vanilla extract and then gradually add the eggs, beating until well combined.

Fold in the flour, baking soda, and salt until combined, then fold in the chocolate, raisins, and oats. Once everything has come together into a dough, spoon it into a rough log shape on a double thickness of parchment paper. Roll this up to make a long roll with the diameter of an average cookie—about 2 to 3 in [5 to 8 cm]. Twist the ends of the paper to roughly seal. The exact shape can be adjusted before cooking so don't worry too much. Put on a plate and refrigerate for at least 1 hour.

Preheat the oven to 350°F [180°C].

Slice off ⅜-in [1-cm] thick circles (however many you want in one sitting!), cutting through the parchment paper. Reshape the disks if they are a little squashed. Place on a greased baking sheet and bake in the preheated oven for 10 minutes, or until golden. Let sit on the sheet for a few moments, then transfer to a wire rack using a spatula and let cool for a few minutes.

Keep the remaining log of cookie dough in the refrigerator or freezer until next time!

APPLE OAT CRUMBLE

This is a lovely adaptation of the traditional baked apple; here all the ingredients are cooked inside it, so they combine to create something really special.

Scant ¼ cup [15 g] rolled oats
2 tsp [10 g] butter
2 tsp [10 g] superfine sugar
½ tsp ground cinnamon
1 medium cooking apple

Preheat the oven to 350˚F [180˚C].

Roughly combine the oats, butter, sugar, and cinnamon in a bowl.

To prepare the apple, using a sharp knife at a 45-degree angle, cut ⅝ in [1.5 cm] from the stalk, around the center, to remove the core and a little of the top. You should end up removing a triangular shape. Then use a teaspoon to remove any remaining core, being careful to keep the base intact.

Lightly score a line around the apple, about one-third down, and score twice from this line to the hole at the top. This will help the apple keep its shape while it bakes.

Stuff the cavity with the oat mixture and bake on a baking sheet in the preheated oven for 20 to 25 minutes, or until the apple is soft but not collapsed, and the topping is crunchy. Remove and serve with a little ice cream or even a little custard.

YOU'LL HAVE MOST OF THESE INGREDIENTS IN YOUR PANTRY ALREADY, SO YOU JUST NEED TO BUY A COOKING APPLE.

INSTANT CHEESECAKE

This is simply a quick assembly job that can include your favorite soft fruit. Just make sure you have enough of the fruit for a good topping, too. This is the kind of recipe that's needed for those special times when you want to be really self-indulgent.

2 graham crackers
1 Tbsp [15 g] cold, salted butter
Scant ¼ cup [25 g] strawberries, plus extra, halved, for topping (or any other soft fruit)
1 heaping Tbsp [15 g] powdered sugar
½ cup [125 g] cold cream cheese (I use the light version), or cold mascarpone

Put the crackers in a freezer bag, seal, and then bash them with a rolling pin or similar to crush them into crumbs. Pour the crumbs into a bowl, add the butter, and rub together to combine them roughly. Spoon them into a ramekin or glass and pat down and compress.

Using a hand blender (or just a fork), blitz together the strawberries and sugar. Combine with the cream cheese and spoon on top of the cracker base in the ramekin. Cover the top with the extra, halved strawberries. Eat immediately or let chill in the refrigerator or freezer for about 20 minutes for a slightly firmer texture.

YOU CAN SWAP PRETTY
MUCH ANY FRUIT FOR
STRAWBERRIES HERE.
BERRIES AND SOFT FRUITS
WORK PARTICULARLY WELL.

FROZEN CUPCAKES

Make 6 of these cupcakes, freeze them, and have one treat weekly—heaven. They're simply delicious and a lifesaver when you come home craving a sweet treat but have no energy to spare!

¾ cup [90 g] self-rising flour
Small pinch of baking powder
Scant ½ cup [90 g] salted butter, softened
½ cup [90 g] superfine sugar
1½ extra-large eggs (or 2 large), at room temperature
½ tsp vanilla extract

Preheat the oven to 350°F [180°C]. Line a muffin or cupcake pan with 6 cupcake liners.

Sift the flour and baking powder into a mixing bowl. Tip the butter and sugar into a second, larger mixing bowl. Beat with a wooden spoon (or an electric beater) for 4 minutes, or until pale, creamy, and light.

Beat the eggs with a fork, then add a dribble at a time to the butter mixture, beating as you go. Don't worry if it splits, just add a little of the flour and mix to bring it back together. Add the vanilla extract.

Add the sifted flour mixture and fold in with a large metal spoon until just mixed. Spoon an equal amount into each cupcake liner using 2 spoons, but don't press it down.

Bake in the oven for 15 to 20 minutes until golden and springy to the touch. Close the oven door slowly if not quite done so they don't collapse. Remove from the oven, take the cupcakes out of the pan, and cool on a rack. Once cooled, freeze these for a month or so, in an airtight container. When required, remove from the freezer and let come to room temperature over a few hours. Top with one of the frostings below.

FROSTINGS

Mascarpone, honey, and preserved ginger frosting (per cupcake)

1 Tbsp mascarpone
1 tsp honey
1 small piece of candied preserved ginger

Combine the mascarpone and honey and pipe or spoon onto a cupcake. Thinly slice the preserved ginger and pop on top of the frosting.

Lime meringue (for 4 cupcakes)

1 large egg white
¼ cup [50 g] superfine sugar
3 tsp lime juice
A little grated lime zest

Using a balloon whisk or electric beater, whisk the egg white until it forms soft peaks. Gradually add the sugar and continue to whisk until it forms hard peaks. Now quickly whisk in the lime juice. Pipe or spoon onto the cupcakes and then blowtorch or stick under a hot broiler until golden. Top with the grated lime zest.

You can leave out the lime, if desired, to make an unflavored meringue, but spread some lemon curd over the cupcake before you top it with the plain meringue.

BREAD AND MAPLE SYRUP PUDDING

What to do with slices of leftover bread? Turn them into the ultimate in sweet comfort food—bread-and-butter pudding! Even if you choose to use package or canned custard this is a winner and the maple syrup makes it irresistible. And it's dead easy …

Butter
1 to 2 slices of bread
Handful of raisins
7 Tbsp [100 ml] ready-made custard
3 tsp maple syrup

Preheat the oven to 350°F [180°C].

Grease a small ovenproof dish. Generously butter the slices of bread and cut the crusts off if desired. Cut into ⅝-in [1.5-cm] "soldiers" or small triangles, if you prefer.

Arrange enough bread in the bottom of the dish to cover it, then sprinkle over the raisins. Pour over the custard and then layer with the leftover bread. Drizzle over the maple syrup. Bake in the preheated oven for 20 minutes, or until piping hot and the bread is crisp and golden.

WE HAVE TWO RECIPES HERE THAT MAKE BRILLIANT USE OF THE SLICED BREAD YOU MIGHT BE STRUGGLING TO GET THROUGH IN THE WEEK.

CINNAMON TOAST

My childhood is filled with food memories, not least this treat, which we used to have in Betty's famous tea rooms in York. Sticky, buttery, crunchy, and with that superb cinnamon spice: dangerously good.

2 Tbsp [25 g] butter, softened
1 Tbsp [20 g] superfine sugar
½ tsp ground cinnamon
A few drops of vanilla extract
  (optional)
2 slices of bread (brown or white)

Preheat the broiler.

Combine the butter, sugar, cinnamon, and vanilla extract.

Lightly toast one side of the bread under the broiler. Once done, spread the untoasted side with the butter mixture, right up to the edges. Place back under the broiler for about 1 minute, making sure the sugar/toast doesn't burn. Remove, slice into "soldiers," and enjoy.

MICROWAVEABLE MUG CAKES

Who wouldn't say yes to a lovely gooey cake that cooks in a couple of minutes? Especially when there are hardly any dishes to wash. This is the perfect dessert for a sweet-tooth, solo indulgence! Eat straight from the mug (or grease the sides beforehand if you want to turn it out).

NUTELLA

3 Tbsp self-rising flour
3 Tbsp Nutella
1 extra-large egg
2 Tbsp milk
1 Tbsp peanut or other
   flavorless oil

Mix all the ingredients in a very large coffee mug (or if you don't have one, divide into 2 smaller mugs, once mixed).

Microwave for between 1 minute 30 seconds and 2 minutes, depending on the strength of your microwave. I found it was just right at 1 minute 45 seconds using my 900W microwave. It should still be a little gooey on top and throughout. Serve with a scoop of vanilla ice cream.

STICKY TOFFEE

1 oz [25 g] dates, pitted
1 decent pinch of baking soda
2 Tbsp boiling water
2 Tbsp [30 g] firmly packed light
   brown sugar
1½ Tbsp [20 g] salted butter,
   softened
½ extra-large egg, beaten
Generous ¼ cup [35 g] self-rising
   flour

Toffee sauce
1 Tbsp [15 g] firmly packed
   brown sugar
1 Tbsp [15 g] butter
2 tsp light corn syrup
Dash of cream (optional)

Chop the dates into small pieces. Combine with the baking soda and boiling water, then set aside.

Cream together the sugar and butter in a bowl with a wooden spoon until light and fluffy. Add the egg and mix. It will split at this point but beating in a large pinch of flour will bring it back together. Fold in the rest of the flour with a large metal spoon, then fold in the date mixture. Spoon the mixture into a medium mug.

Microwave for 3 minutes 30 seconds at 600W, or until a metal skewer comes out clean when inserted in the middle of the dessert.

Meanwhile, make the toffee sauce by combining the ingredients in a saucepan, melting over gentle heat and boiling for a minute or two. Finally, add the cream, if desired.

I like to prick the dessert all over with a skewer, once cooked, and then pour over the sauce. Let sit for a minute because it (and the mug) will be REALLY hot.

CAKE FOR ONE? YES PLEASE! CHOOSE FROM TWO FLAVORS AND TRY THEM WHEN YOU NEED A SWEET HIT.

INDEX

A

apples: apple oat crumble 177
  chops, chorizo and cheese 89
  pork, apple, and sage potato cakes
   102
  quick applesauce 89
  roast pork belly 100–1
arancini 136
artichoke heart, basil, and
  mozzarella tart 164
Asian chicken salad 14
Asian slaw 62
asparagus: smoky duck breast
  with griddled asparagus 46
avocados: Nordic smoked salmon
  143
  teriyaki nachos 17

B

baked beans: quick cassoulet 98
BBQ beef rib sandwich 67
BBQ beef ribs 67
BBQ chicken burger 28
BBQ duck rolls with hot sauce 53
beans 9
  chipotle steak and cheese
   quesadillas 66
  lamb and feta salad 120
  lamb steaks with rosemary
   cannellini beans 120
  quick cassoulet 98
beef 10
  BBQ beef rib sandwich 67
  BBQ beef ribs 67
  beef and ale pie 58
  bubble and squeak cakes 60
  chipotle steak and cheese
   quesadillas 66
  cottage pie 73
  ginger beef burger with Asian
   slaw 62
  hot beef sandwich 78
  miso steak and chili sweet potato
   66
  Philly cheesesteak sandwich 56
  pho 80
  posh beef and tatties 72
  roast beef 74–5
  spag bol 76
  spaghetti and meatballs 64
  spicy stir-fried beef 68
  steak and roasted red pepper
   salad 57

beer: beef and ale pie 58
  beer and orange chicken 14
  mussels in beer 140
beet: beet and lamb 114
  lamb and mint burger 114
black fungus, sweet chili pork
  stir-fry with 86
bread: BBQ duck rolls with hot
  sauce 53
  bread and maple syrup pudding
   182
  cinnamon toast 183
  creamy leek and peas on warm
   ciabatta 150
  fast fish pie 138
  horseradish toasts 57
  minty lamb sandwich 124
  shepherd's pie 110
  see also sandwiches
breakfast hash 92
broccoli: egg fried rice with garlic
  broccoli 70
bubble and squeak cakes 60
burgers: BBQ chicken
  burger 28
  ginger beef burger with Asian
   slaw 62
  lamb and mint burger 114
butternut squash: roast butternut
  squash dip 148
  roast butternut squash with
   ricotta and arugula on gnocchi
   148

C

cabbage: Asian slaw 62
  bubble and squeak cakes 60
cakes: frozen cupcakes 180
  Nutella mug cakes 184
  sticky toffee mug cakes 184
cannellini beans: lamb and feta
  salad 120
  lamb steaks with rosemary
   cannellini beans 120
caramel: sticky toffee mug cakes
  184
  sticky toffee popcorn 174
carrots: Asian slaw 62
cassoulet, quick 98
cheese: artichoke heart, basil, and
  mozzarella tart 164
   chipotle steak and cheese
    quesadillas 66
  chorizo, feta, and roasted red
   pepper omelet 91
  chops, chorizo and cheese 89
  creamy pasta frittata 26

duck, feta, and spinach
  phyllo pie 50
easy arancini 136
eggplant chicken parmigiana 33
fast Turkish pizza 171
griddled scallion tart 162
lamb and feta salad 120
lamb, feta, and hummus pita
  127
leek and pea Glamorgan sausages
  150
pasta with roasted peppers and
  goat cheese 170
pecorino popcorn 174
Philly cheesesteak sandwich 56
roast butternut squash dip 148
roast butternut squash with
  ricotta and arugula on gnocchi
  148
cheesecake 178
chicken 10
  Asian chicken salad 14
  baked lemon chicken legs 32
  BBQ chicken burger 28
  beer and orange chicken 14
  chicken and chorizo pasta bowl
   30
  chicken and leek pasta 24
  chicken and tarragon potato cake
   37
  chicken saag curry 18
  chicken sandwiches 36
  chicken soup 38
  chicken teriyaki 16
  chicken tikka kabobs 20
  eggplant chicken parmigiana 33
  flattened griddled chicken with
   couscous 22
  Moroccan salad 22
  roast chicken 34–5
  teriyaki nachos 17
chicken livers: chicken liver wrap 23
  liver pâté 23
chile: chili sweet potato wedges 28
  five-spice duck legs with chili
   sweet potato mash 42
  miso steak and chili sweet potato
   66
  spicy stir-fried beef 68
  sweet chili pork stir fry with black
   fungus 86
Chinese slow-cooked pork 88
chipotle steak and cheese
  quesadillas 66
chocolate: cookie rolls 176
  Nutella mug cakes 184
  ultimate chocolate milkshake 28

chorizo: chicken and chorizo pasta bowl 30
chops, chorizo and cheese 89
chorizo and sweet potato soup 90
chorizo, feta, and roasted red pepper omelet 91
chorizo fishcakes 132
cod and chorizo with pesto potatoes and peas 130
quick cassoulet 98
cilantro: harissa pork with mango and cilantro couscous 84
lentil, coconut, and cilantro pâté 151
cinnamon toast 183
cod: chorizo fishcakes 132
cod and chorizo with pesto potatoes and peas 130
cookie rolls 176
cottage pie 73
couscous: flattened griddled chicken with couscous 22
harissa pork with mango and cilantro couscous 84
Moroccan salad 22
rack of lamb with couscous and griddled eggplant 108
cream cheese: cheesecake 178
liver pâté 23
Philly cheesesteak sandwich 56
crumble, apple oat 177
cucumber: tofu and cucumber salad 158
cupcakes, frozen 180
curry: chicken liver wrap 23
chicken saag curry 18
quick shrimp curry 134
Thai lentil dhal 151
custard: bread and maple syrup pudding 182

D
dhal, Thai lentil 151
dip, roast butternut squash 148
duck: BBQ duck rolls with hot sauce 53
duck, feta, and spinach phyllo pie 50
duck legs in plum sauce with Asian greens 44
duck ragu 45
five-spice duck legs with chili sweet potato mash 42
lettuce wraps with shredded duck and hoisin sauce 42
roast duck 48-9

smoky duck breast with griddled asparagus 46
Vietnamese duck salad 47

E
eggplant: eggplant and tomato fusilli 152
eggplant chicken parmigiana 33
Mexican salad 157
miso eggplant salad 154
rack of lamb with couscous and griddled eggplant 108
ratatouille 166
veggie fajitas 157
eggs: chorizo, feta, and roasted red pepper omelet 91
creamy pasta frittata 26
egg fried rice with garlic broccoli 70
spaghetti carbonara 94

F
fajitas, veggie 157
fava beans: warm lamb salad 108
fish 11
fast fish pie 138
see also cod, salmon etc
fishcakes: chorizo fishcakes 132
10 minute fish cakes 139
five-spice duck legs with chili sweet potato mash 42
frankfurters: pork and split pea soup 104
frittata, creamy pasta 26
frostings 180
fusilli, eggplant, and tomato 152

G
garbanzo beans: garbanzo and potato soup, spicy 156
Lebanese style garbanzo salad 156
garlic and lemon chops 115
ginger: ginger beef burger with Asian slaw 62
mascarpone, honey, and preserved ginger frosting 180
Glamorgan sausages, leek, and pea 150
gnocchi: roast butternut squash with ricotta and arugula on gnocchi 148
goat cheese: pasta with roasted peppers and goat cheese 170
green beans: griddled shrimp with lemony green bean salad 135

H
haddock: fast fish pie 138
ham: maple-glazed ham steak 94
spaghetti carbonara 94
harissa: garbonza and potato soup, spicy 156
harissa pork with mango and cilantro couscous 84
herbs 8
hoisin sauce, lettuce wraps with shredded duck and 42
horseradish: horseradish toasts 57
salmon packages 144
smoked mackerel pâté with a kick 142
hummus: lamb, feta, and hummus pita 127

I
ice cream: ultimate chocolate milkshake 28

K
kabobs, chicken tikka 20
kofta wrap 112

L
lamb 10-11
beet and lamb 114
garlic and lemon chops 115
kofta wrap 112
lamb and feta salad 120
lamb and mint burger 114
lamb, feta, and hummus pita 127
lamb potato cakes 118
lamb steaks with rosemary cannellini beans 120
lamb stir-fry 115
lamb stroganoff 125
minty lamb sandwich 124
one-pot lamb stew 116
rack of lamb with couscous and griddled eggplant 108
shepherd's pie 110
slow-cooked lamb shanks with olives and polenta 123
spring broth with lamb 117
tikka lamb chops 118
warm lamb salad 108
Lebanese style chickpea salad 156
leeks: chicken and leek pasta 24
creamy leek and peas on warm ciabatta 150
leek and pea Glamorgan sausages 150

lemon: baked lemon chicken legs 32
  garlic and lemon chops 115
lentils: lentil, coconut, and cilantro pâté 151
  sausage and lentil stew 93
  Thai lentil dhal 151
lettuce wraps with shredded duck and hoisin sauce 42
lime meringue 180
linguine: creamy smoked salmon pasta 143
  mussel linguine 140
liver see chicken livers

M
macaroni: chicken soup 38
  ratatouille and pasta soup 168
mackerel see smoked mackerel
mangoes: harissa pork with mango and cilantro couscous 84
  Vietnamese duck salad 47
maple syrup: bread and maple syrup pudding 182
  maple-glazed ham 94
mascarpone, honey, and preserved ginger frosting 180
meatballs: sausage meatballs and pasta 96
  spaghetti and meatballs 64
meringue, lime 180
Mexican salad 157
milkshake, ultimate chocolate 28
minty lamb sandwich 124
miso eggplant salad 154
miso steak and chili sweet potato 66
Moroccan salad 22
mushrooms: beef and ale pie 58
  beer and orange chicken 14
  breakfast hash 92
  lamb stroganoff 125
  sweet chili pork stir-fry with black fungus 86
mussels: mussel linguine 140
  mussels in beer 140
mustard 9

N
nachos, teriyaki 17
noodles: pho 80
Nordic smoked salmon 143
Nutella mug cakes 184

O
oats: apple oat crumble 177
  cookie rolls 176

oils 8
olives: slow-cooked lamb shanks with olives and polenta 123
omelet: chorizo, feta, and roasted red pepper 91
one-pot lamb stew 116
onions, spiced 118
orange: beer and orange chicken 14
  Moroccan salad 22

P
paella, seafood 136
pak choi: duck legs in plum sauce with Asian greens 44
pasta: eggplant and tomato fusilli 152
  chicken and chorizo pasta bowl 30
  chicken and leek pasta 24
  chicken soup 38
  creamy pasta frittata 26
  creamy smoked salmon pasta 143
  duck ragu 45
  mussel linguine 140
  pasta with roasted peppers and goat cheese 170
  ratatouille and pasta soup 168
  sausage and mustard pasta 93
  sausage meatballs and pasta 96
  spag bol 76
  spaghetti and meatballs 64
  spaghetti carbonara 94
pâtés: lentil, coconut, and cilantro pâté 151
  liver pâté 23
  simple salmon pâté 145
peas: creamy leek and peas on warm ciabatta 150
  leek and pea Glamorgan sausages 150
peas, split: pork and split pea soup 104
pecorino popcorn 174
peppers: chorizo, feta, and roasted red pepper omelet 91
  fast Turkish pizza 171
  lamb and feta salad 120
  pasta with roasted peppers and goat cheese 170
  steak and roasted red pepper salad 57
pesto: cod and chorizo with pesto potatoes and peas 130
Philly cheesesteak sandwich 56
pho 80
phyllo pie: duck, feta, and spinach 50

pickles 16
pies: beef and ale pie 58
  cottage pie 73
  duck, feta, and spinach phyllo pie 50
  fast fish pie 138
  shepherd's pie 110
pita, lamb, feta, and hummus 127
pizza, fast Turkish 171
plum sauce, duck legs in 44
polenta, slow-cooked lamb shanks with olives and 123
popcorn 174
pork 10
  Chinese slow-cooked pork 88
  chops, chorizo and cheese 89
  harissa pork with mango and cilantro couscous 84
  pork and split pea soup 104
  pork, apple, and sage potato cakes 102
  pork belly salad with spicy sesame dressing 88
  pork sandwich with quick applesauce 89
  roast pork belly 100–1
  satay pork sandwich 103
  sweet chili pork stir-fry with black fungus 86
posh beef and tatties 72
potatoes: baked lemon chicken legs 32
  breakfast hash 92
  bubble and squeak cakes 60
  chicken and tarragon potato cake 37
  chickpea and potato soup, spicy 156
  chorizo fishcakes 132
  cod and chorizo with pesto potatoes and peas 130
  cottage pie 73
  lamb potato cakes 118
  maple-glazed ham 94
  one-pot lamb stew 116
  pork, apple, and sage potato cakes 102
  posh beef and tatties 72
  roast chicken 34–5
  salmon packages 144
  sausage and mash 92
  smoked mackerel Niçoise 142
  10 minute fish cakes 139
  tikka lamb chops 118

Q
quesadillas, chipotle steak and cheese 66

R
ragu, duck 45
ratatouille 166
  ratatouille and pasta soup 168
rice 11
  easy arancini 136
  egg fried rice with garlic broccoli 70
  seafood paella 136
  spicy stir-fried beef 68
ricotta: roast butternut squash dip 148
  roast butternut squash with ricotta and arugula on gnocchi 148
rutabaga: maple-glazed ham 94

S
salads: Asian chicken salad 14
  Asian slaw 62
  griddled shrimp with lemony green bean salad 135
  lamb and feta salad 120
  Lebanese style chickpea salad 156
  Mexican salad 157
  miso eggplant salad 154
  Moroccan salad 22
  pork belly salad with spicy sesame dressing 88
  smoked mackerel Niçoise 142
  steak and roasted red pepper salad 57
  tofu and cucumber salad 158
  Vietnamese duck salad 47
  warm lamb salad 108
salmon: salmon packages 144
  simple salmon pâté 145
salt n' pepper tofu 160
sandwiches: BBQ beef rib sandwich 67
  chicken sandwiches 36
  hot beef sandwich 78
  lamb, feta, and hummus pita 127
  Philly cheesesteak sandwich 56
  pork sandwich with quick apple-sauce 89
  satay pork sandwich 103
satay pork sandwich 103
sausages: breakfast hash 92
  leek and pea Glamorgan sausages 150
  pork and split pea soup 104

quick cassoulet 98
  sausage and lentil stew 93
  sausage and mash 92
  sausage and mustard pasta 93
  sausage meatballs and pasta 96
  see also chorizo
scallions: griddled scallion tart 162
seafood paella 136
shepherd's pie 110
shrimp: griddled shrimp with lemony green bean salad 135
  quick shrimp curry 134
smoked mackerel: smoked mackerel pâté with a kick 142
  smoked mackerel Niçoise 142
smoked salmon: creamy smoked salmon pasta 143
  Nordic smoked salmon 143
smoky duck breast with griddled asparagus 46
soups: chicken soup 38
  chorizo and sweet potato soup 90
  garbanzo and potato soup, spicy 156
  pho 80
  pork and split pea soup 104
  ratatouille and pasta soup 168
  spring broth with lamb 117
spaghetti: spag bol 76
  spaghetti and meatballs 64
  spaghetti carbonara 94
spices 8
spinach: chicken saag curry 18
  duck, feta, and spinach phyllo pie 50
split peas: pork and split pea soup 104
spring broth with lamb 117
squash *see* butternut squash
steak and roasted red pepper salad 57
stews: one-pot lamb stew 116
  sausage and lentil stew 93
  slow-cooked lamb shanks with olives and polenta 123
sticky toffee mug cakes 184
sticky toffee popcorn 174
storage 10–11
strawberries: cheesecake 178
sugar 9
sweet chili pork stir-fry with black fungus 86
sweet potatoes: chili sweet potato wedges 28
  chorizo and sweet potato soup 90

five-spice duck legs with chili sweet potato mash 42
  miso steak and chili sweet potato 66

T
tarts: artichoke heart, basil, and mozzarella tart 164
  griddled scallion tart 162
teriyaki nachos 17
Thai lentil dhal 151
tikka lamb chops 118
toast: cinnamon toast 183
  horseradish toasts 57
toffee sauce 184
tofu: salt n' pepper tofu 160
  tofu and cucumber salad 158
tomatoes: eggplant and tomato fusilli 152
  chicken saag curry 18
  duck ragu 45
  mussel linguine 140
  ratatouille 166
  sausage meatballs and pasta 96
  slow-cooked lamb shanks with olives and polenta 123
  spag bol 76
  tomato sauce 64
tortillas: chipotle steak and cheese quesadillas 66
  veggie fajitas 157

V
vegetables: ratatouille 166
  spring broth with lamb 117
  see also eggplants, peppers, etc.
veggie fajitas 157
Vietnamese duck salad 47
vinegars 8

W
wine: duck ragu 45
  sausage and lentil stew 93
  slow-cooked lamb shanks with olives and polenta 123
wraps: chicken liver wrap 23
  kofta wrap 112
  lettuce wraps with shredded duck and hoisin sauce 42
  Nordic smoked salmon 143
  veggie fajitas 157

ACKNOWLEDGMENTS

A huge thank you to all these lovely people ...

For making the book look beautiful: Céline Hughes, Gemma Hayden, Helen Lewis, Lisa Linder, Fiona Kennedy, Emily Jonzen, Polly Webb-Wilson, Aya Nishimura.

For help and amazing support: Felicity Blunt, Emma Herdman, and Jane O'Shea.

To my family and friends: Dad for being chief taster and general hero. My sister Polly and brother Tom for always being there for me. My terrific tasters Yuley and Louise. Mickey, the cat, helpfully cleaning up anything I dropped on the floor.

In memory of my wonderful mom, who gave me the love of food and constantly inspired and supported me in every way. You are missed and thought of every day, especially when I'm in the kitchen. This is for you.

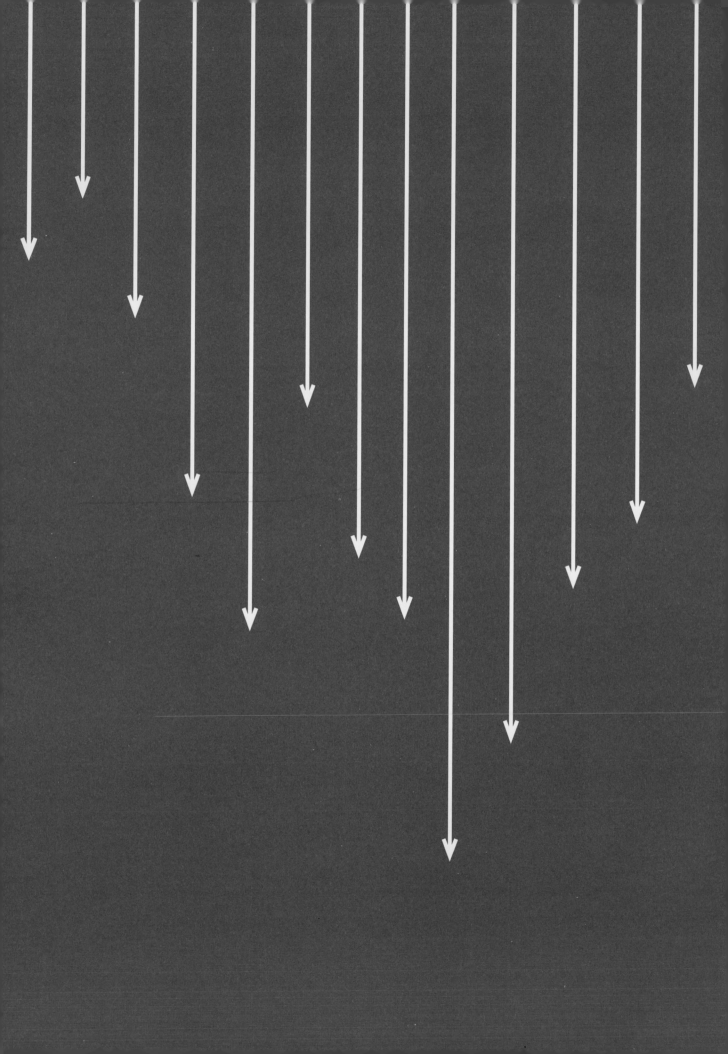